COLOMB
CANADIA
Quiz
BOOK

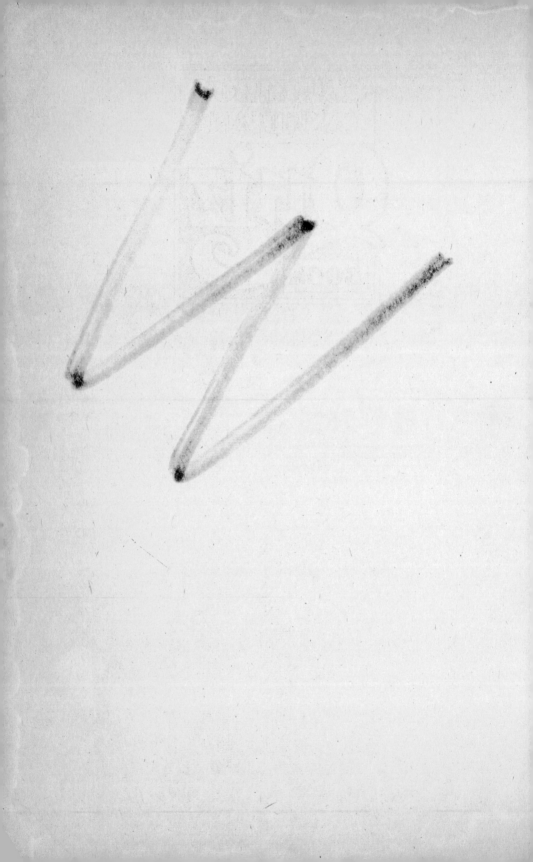

COLOMBO'S CANADIANA Quiz BOOK

John Robert Colombo

Western Producer Prairie Books
Saskatoon, Saskatchewan

Book Design by Warren Clark, GDL

Printed and bound in Canada by
Modern Press ⟨logo⟩ 1
Saskatoon, Saskatchewan

Western Producer Prairie Books publications
are produced and manufactured in the middle of
western Canada by a unique publishing venture owned
by a group of prairie farmers who are members of Saskatchewan
Wheat Pool. From the first book in 1954, a reprint of a serial
originally carried in the weekly newspaper, *The Western Producer,*
to the book before you now, the tradition of
providing enjoyable and informative reading
for all Canadians is continued.

The publisher acknowledges the support
received for this publication from the
Canada Council.

Canadian Cataloguing in Publication Data

Colombo, John Robert, 1936-
Colombo's Canadiana quiz book

ISBN 0-88833-114-2

1. Canada — Miscellanea. 2. Questions and answers.
I. Title. II. Title: Canadiana quiz book.
FC61.C64 1983   971'.002   C83-091435-8
F1008.3.C64 1983

**IN MEMORY OF
TERRY FOX
(1958-1981)
"Dreams Are Made If People Try"**

CONTENTS

PREFACE

This volume is a general-knowledge, Canadiana quiz book. It focuses on those people, places, and things that are characteristic of this country, if not unique to it. The book takes an entire country and a heterogeneous group of disparate peoples as its subject. Although that country is among the largest in the world, and among the oldest in the United Nations, Canadians too often see themselves as little people in a big world and young people in an old world. Hence what they think they should know about their country is limited.

For this reason knowledge of Canada is regarded as a specialty subject. The purpose of this book is to examine and expand that specialty — to increase one's knowledge of the country and to deepen one's awareness and appreciation of the human condition here. J. Castell Hopkins's comment — "Canada only needs to be known in order to be great" — remains as true today as when the Toronto editor first said it in 1901. I like the sentiment and the sense, for it makes greatness contingent upon the most important form of knowledge: self-knowledge. The quotation implies that Canadians will become finer and more fulfilled as a people as they become more aware of themselves and the world in which they live.

To that end this book asks a lot of questions. Indeed, it asks over 2,000 questions, arranged in some 165 sets, organized by forty-one categories. There have been other Canadiana quiz books, but this one is by far the largest and the only one systematically organized. Although the subject of the book is ostensibly Canada and Canadians, the book is really about history, society, invention, people, about us.

Answering the questions here will challenge the average Canadian and add to his or her self-knowledge. A glance at the questions will show that they vary in difficulty. Some require more background knowledge than others. Some impart more information than others. With a few calculated exceptions here and there, the questions (in the body of the book) and the answers (in the back of the book) come from the mainstream of contemporary Canadian life. My belief is that the average educated Canadian should know such things, for this is what it means to be culturally Canadian. As Harold Adams Innis noted, "Nationalism provides the only basis for internationalism." If we do not understand and appreciate the conditions that created us, how are we to understand and appreciate the conditions that created the rest of the world?

Although I believe national knowledge is essential for well-being, I am not naive enough to limit such knowledge to the questions and answers in this book. Certainly, contemporary Canadian life is broader than the Canadianism of this book. Yet to bring that Canadianness into focus, it has been found necessary to bear exclusively upon the Canadian — as distinct from the North American or English-language — experience. The ideal question in a Canadiana quiz book could be answered only by a Canadian. It is also true that no questionee will be able to answer *all* the questions set by the questioner. (Indeed, the questioner could not recall the answers to a good many of them even a few days after setting them!) But everyone should be able to work out the answers to a good many of them, and what is not already known could be learned.

The realization of the book's aim is based on the concept of "deep fun" and "facts with fun." The phrase "facts with fun" was used in connection with an early CBC-TV show, "Tabloid," which caught a lightness of spirit that is so admirable. I do not know who first used the phrase "deep fun," but it catches in two words the notion I cherish that learning is a happy and joyous experience, though occasionally tempered by drudgery. This quiz book minimizes the drudge-work (after all, the question-setter did all that!) and maximizes the element of challenge.

Who created the first quiz? The *Oxford English Dictionary* gives "origin obscure" for the etymology of the word. Jane Austen used the noun *quiz* in 1782 to mean "an odd-looking person," and this obsolete meaning persists in the adjective *quizzical* — "curious, peculiar." Thereafter the word has been used in two senses: one who asks questions, the act of asking questions.

There is a story told about James Daly, an eighteenth-century Dublin theater manager, who wagered with friends that he could create a brand-new word and make it the talk of the town. They bet he could not, so he dreamt up the word *quiz*. One night he hired men to paint these four letters on walls and fences all over Dublin. The next morning, Dubliners "quizzed" one another about the meaning of the graffiti, and Daly won his wager.

Or so the story goes. Eric Partridge noted that the word is similar in sound to the Latin tag *Quid est?* (meaning "What is?") and that the sound and sense linger in modern English in such words as "in*quis*itor" and "in*quis*itive." Roy Ward Dickson, known across Canada for his numerous quiz programs on radio and television, claimed he was the first user of the word (which he spelled with two zeds, to match *jazz* and *fuzz*) in its modern context. He did so on "Professor Dick and His Question Box," heard by radio listeners in the Toronto area on 15 May 1935. As Dickson billed himself as the "King of Quiz" — or "Quizz" — his claim must be taken seriously. "The value of a quiz as a source of entertainment," noted Dickson, "depends on a number of basic factors."

Firstly, it must be interesting to a significant proportion of the general public. A quiz on computer technology, or on native customs on the island of Celebes, might provide half an hour's amusement for a gathering of electronics experts or of anthropologists, but it would not attract the vast majority of people to their television sets or bookshops. So the subjects must be selected to provide the greatest appeal to the widest audience. Secondly, it must be informative, challenging and thought-provoking. It would be an affront to the contestant merely to attempt to boost his ego with a bunch of ridiculously simple questions. When someone fails to answer a question, the disappointment should be offset by the satisfaction of increasing his store of knowledge . . . and, of course, an interesting quiz can serve to make us remember what we thought we had forgotten. Thirdly, fairness is essential. Quite apart from cases where a prize is being offered, the rules must be understood and adhered to, and the wording of the material should not be deliberately misleading or unnecessarily ambiguous — unless this is done to provide amusement and change of pace, with the agreement of the contestants.

Accuracy, too, is vital and goes hand in hand with fairness. A quiz, at whatever level and in whatever context, is a game, and the experience should be a pleasurable one or it becomes pointless. Doubts and dissatisfaction arising from inaccuracies in the wording of questions, or in the material against which a player's answers are judged, do little to enhance the enjoyment.

How educational is the quiz? I put this question to Sandy Stewart. An authority on the history of Canadian radio and television, and veteran producer of audience-participation programs for CBC-TV, Stewart is the long-time executive producer of such popular and once-popular quiz programs as "Reach for the Top." He has some thoughtful ideas about quizzes and what they accomplish.

Quizzes have always been popular. They probably grew out of the educational situation, Bible instruction in particular. Teach and test, teach and test. This is really the only method of instruction, and it is ancient. It appeals to today's television-viewers — look at the popularity of daytime television give-away shows (which are not really quiz shows but ways of giving away money and goods as prizes).

Canadians are great quiz-show producers. We produce our share of game shows too, but broadcast regulations have limited the amount of prize money that can be given away. We have to our credit a great number of fine quiz programs on radio and television. "Treasure Trail" was immensely popular in its day. "Front Page Challenge," which has a strong element of quiz, is one of the longest-running shows on Canadian television, and for good reason.

Are quiz programs educational? Until recently I was inclined to answer no. For one thing, there are right and wrong answers to the questions. No gray areas are permitted. The quiz-master is after the answer he has on the page of the script in front of him. He hopes it is the correct answer. At best it is "what is generally regarded as" the best answer.

Another reason quiz programs are probably not educational is that the recall factor is so small. So much information is being heard, the answer deemed correct flits by so quickly, that hours after he has heard it he has forgotten it.

Therefore I would be inclined to answer no, they are not really educational in their own right. However, as the result of audience surveys taken with "Reach for the Top," I have had to revise or modify my earlier opinion. People who watch quiz programs think of them as educational, and so do participants on them. Many educators rate them highly as encouraging learning. So I now answer that question with a qualified yes. Quiz programs are educational, if only for two reasons.

The first reason is that they work as a normalizing factor in the world of learning. By asking a certain type of question about a certain body of knowledge — "What is the tallest mountain in the world?" — they imply that the answers to such questions are worth knowing. So quizzes stake out a body of knowledge — a body of information that can be tested — then declare that body to be the norm of what the average educated person should know. The second way in which they are educational is that they reinforce cultural values. They do this be their very existence.

Because valuable radio or television time, or space on a library shelf, is taken up with quiz programs and books, one is subconsciously impressed by the fact that they must have social value. Therefore, participation — if only by watching or listening or reading — is important. When a question is asked, everyone says, if only to himself, "I know the answer to that question" or "I should know the answer" or "I once knew the answer." This in itself is instructive and educational.

There is, of course, no room for value judgments or interpretations in the quiz format. The only way you can ask a religious-knowledge question is by prefacing it with a qualification like "According to the King James translation of the Bible. . . ." Sex and partisan politics are out of the question. Then there is the whole business of specialty. Some people — men usually — know everything there is to know about sports achievements. Other people cannot tell a batting average from a bowling score. Trivia questions are always appealing but ever unfair. As someone once said, an easy question is one the player can answer; a difficult question is one he cannot answer.

A good quiz-master, by the way he presents the question, by the rapport he establishes with the questionee, may help that person to answer a question he never believed he could answer. He inspires confidence. Similarly, a well-worded question, unlike a poorly worded one, often elicits buried knowledge. Some emcees create an extraordinary climate conducive to recall. The experience may be intensely dramatic.

What is most basic to quiz? Dominance. Yes, dominance. The questioner tries to dominate the questionee. Panelists compete among themselves. Members of teams try to outshine other members. The audience challenges questionees to perform well, and each member of the audience quizzes and challenges himself.

The audience likes to come out on top now and then. The plumber in the audience can answer the question about wrench sizes that the future Rhodes Scholar on "Reach for the Top" missed. The question about dress patterns may flummox the panelist but delight the housewife who knows all about the subject.

So quiz is another word for verbal dominance.

Two professors of English at the University of Toronto, Ann and John Robson, also insist on the importance of word games in their book, *Word Games for Families Who Are Still Speaking to Each Other.*

Everyone learns from word games. We are among the many who have been complaining that, in the past decade, schools have not been sufficiently concerned about the mystery and mastery of language. In fact, thinking about the school non-system tends to make us incoherent, so we use these games both to aid our coherence and to make us forget our complaints. We find that they develop vocabulary, increase semantic and syntactic control, and stimulate logic and imagination.

As far as kinds of questions are concerned, this quiz book resembles a box of all sorts. There is something here for everyone. There are Multiple Choice questions. Mix and Match questions. Fill in the Blanks. True and False. Identifications. Correspondences. Recognitions. There are even puzzle questions — Word Mazes, Words from Letters, and Scramblings. It is possible to know nothing about Canada and yet work out the answers to some of the puzzles.

Questions differ in kind but also in difficulty. Some demand more in the way of information; others, more in the way of ingenuity, patience, or luck. Just as some questions demand more, some answerers know more. It is impossible for any one questioner to know what any one answerer knows. My favorite way of expressing this is: one man's trivia is another man's treasure. Or to use Sandy Stewart's formulation, a trivial question is one you can't answer. Everyone has an area of expertise, but areas do not necessarily overlap. Over and above that there are general-interest questions where the level of difficulty may be determined but only indirectly measured. Generally, I have avoided specialist questions in favor of general-interest ones.

So this book could be regarded as programmed learning, for it "corrects" the student. Alas, it does so by telling him the right or correct answer, so no further "learning" is required. Yet it can be used in a number of ways.

There is one thing the user of this book must not do if he is to "play the game." He must not turn repeatedly from the questions in the body of the book to the answers at the back. It is best to play with pen and paper handy, to jot down the correct answers. Once a set of questions has been answered, only then turn to the back of the book for the answers. If the questionee trusts to his memory, he will find he is repeatedly turning to the answers; once there, he cannot resist glancing at the up-and-coming answer, thereby prejudicing his opportunity to answer the next question unprompted. So the best thing to do is to keep pencil and paper handy — and resist the temptation to answer the questions piecemeal.

Some sets will take longer to complete than others. Indeed, some sets may be completed correctly only with some research — dipping into the daily newspaper, visiting the reference section of the nearest local library, conversing with knowledgeable friends. But there are no time-limits. What is being tested is knowledge, not understanding, though it is unlikely one will have much of the former without some of the latter.

A system of handicapping will permit younger players to compete against older players, or generalists against specialists, by compensating for inequalities in knowledge and experience. Grant the novice some points with which to begin; double the number of earned points; or permit two novices to work as a team against one senior player. There are a few systems of handicapping.

Time may be made a factor in the play when two or more people "play the game" by competing against each other either singly or in teams. Before the advent of permissive education, teachers encouraged intellectual competition among students by conducting "round-robins" and "spelling bees." Students would take turns answering questions one after the other in a round-robin. When a question is incorrectly answered, the next student has the opportunity to answer it. This continues and the student with the greatest number of points wins. In a spelling bee, the students are divided into two equal groups. Students who fail to answer correctly drop out, and the group with at least one member still standing wins. These are but two ways in which two or more players may "play the book."

ACKNOWLEDGMENTS

Innumerable acknowledgments are in order and are made with gratitude. I was encouraged every step of the way by my wife, Ruth Colombo. Many contributions were made by Philip Singer and Michael Richardson of the North York Public Library. Librarians at the Metropolitan Toronto Library and the CBC Reference Library were extremely helpful. Specific assistance was tendered by Joel Bonn, Ron Butchard, John Miller, Stan Obodiac, Morris C. Shumiatcher, and Sandy Stewart. I benefitted from my correspondence with the late Roy Ward Dickson. I cherish my appearance on the panel of the original radio version of "Fighting Words" in 1958, under the inimitable Nathan Cohen. More recently, David Milligan and Michael Snook of CBC Radio commissioned a quiz for "The Entertainers." Len Sher did the same for "Arts National." For CBC-TV, Dick Donovan was producer of the mini-series "Colombo's Quotes," and Sandy Stewart was executive producer of "Mastermind" for which I served as chief question-setter. As well, I am grateful to the staff of Western Producer Prairie Books who saw the educational value of this book. Along with the freelance editor, Diane Mew, and Paul Hack, among others, they saved me from not a few errors. The credits for the photographs appear in the Answers section. Let me conclude by assuring the reader that it is a lot easier to write questions like these than it is to answer them!

1. Hail!

Greetings to the reader follow in both official languages, in two of the native tongues, and in Esperanto. Match the words of greeting (left) with their respective languages (right).

1. Ahneen!   A. Algonkian.
2. Ai!   B. English.
3. Hello!   C. Esperanto.
4. Salut!   D. French.
5. Saluton!   E. Inuktitut.

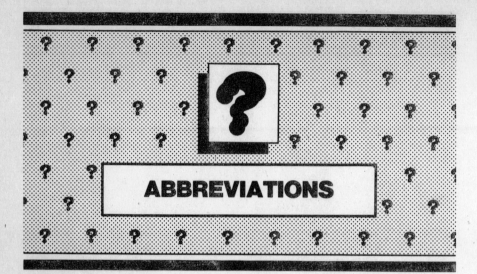

2. Abbreviations

Abbreviations are all around us. Short forms are so common that we use them without thinking about it. Mr. for "Mister," St. for "Saint" or "Street," TV for "television" ... the list is endless. Here are some common Canadian abbreviations, the majority of which would baffle any non-Canadian. How many can you expand and explain?

1. ARCT.
2. CAF.
3. CBC
4. CDN.
5. CLC.
6. CN.
7. CP.
8. CRTC.
9. CTV.
10. FRSC.
11. NDP.
12. NHL.
13. OC.
14. QC.
15. SRC.
16. UCC.
17. W5.

3. Acronyms

Most abbreviations are sounded out letter by letter (like CN, in the last set of questions). But some abbreviations, pronounced like words in their own rights, are called acronyms. Here are some acronyms that are common across the country yet would defeat the outsider. Pronounce them and identify them by expanding them.

1. CAATs.
2. CANDU.
3. CEGEPs.
4. CIDA.
5. CUPE.
6. CUSO.
7. FIRA.
8. NATO.
9. NORAD.

AGRICULTURE

4. Agricultural Statistics

How much do you know about the facts and figures of Canadian agriculture? Test your knowledge with the following questions.

1. What percentage of Canada's total area is farmland?
   - A. 7%
   - B. 17%
   - C. 27%
   - D. 37%

2. What percentage of Canada's farmland is privately owned by family farmers?
   - A. 57%
   - B. 67%
   - C. 77%
   - D. 87%

3. There are 1.2 million ha (3 million acres) of potentially arable land and large expanses of grazing land north of latitude 55°, that is, north of Flin Flon, Man. How many commercial farms are there amid these 1.2 million ha?
   - A. 0
   - B. 30
   - C. 300
   - D. 3,000

4. What share of Canada's farm cash receipts are generated by exports?
   - A. 20%
   - B. 30%
   - C. 50%
   - D. 60%

5. Of the world's people Canadians spend the second lowest percentage of their disposable income on food. What percentage is it?
   A. 7.1%
   B. 17.1%
   C. 27.1%
   D. 37.1%

6. Which province has the largest number of commercial livestock farms and is second only in the number of dairy farms?

7. All the hens in commercial production in Canada in 1979 laid an astonishing number of eggs. How many did they lay (in dozens)?
   A. 1 million dozen.
   B. 20 million dozen.
   C. 460 million dozen.
   D. One and one half billion dozen.

8. Which three provinces contain 75% of the farmland of Canada?

9. In these three provinces, what is by far the largest single crop.

10. Which province is first in wheat production and grows two-thirds of Canada's wheat?

11. From 1941 to 1976 the number of farms in western Canada changed dramatically. What was the change?
    A. 20% increase
    B. 25% increase
    C. 45% decrease
    D. 75% decrease

12. They say a Russian peasant can produce enough food to feed three Russian generals. How many Canadians can each Canadian farmer feed?
    A. 5
    B. 15
    C. 35
    D. 55

---

5. The Greatest Good

"To be born on a farm is the greatest good that can befall a human being," wrote Peter McArthur. "To live on a farm and enjoy all that it has to offer is the greatest good that can be attained by a poet or a philosopher." Here is a set of questions on that "greatest good."

1. Which province is sometimes called "The Million-Acre Farm"?
2. Traditionally, Quebec has small mixed-farming operations. Now well over half of commercial farms in that province are classed as _____ farms.
3. What agricultural nickname has been adopted by the town of Tisdale, Saskatchewan?
4. Which is the most important fruit grown in Canada?
5. Which is the most important vegetable produced in Canada?
6. For which province are potatoes the leading crop?
7. Which are the so-called tender tree fruits?

8. Which region of Ontario accounts for most of Canada's tender tree fruits and grapes?

9. Which province is Canada's largest producer of apples, and which region of that province is noted for such tree fruits as peaches, plums, and cherries?

10. Does the Canadian Wheat Board, established in 1935, market wheat grown in Ontario?

11. Marquis wheat, the disease-resistant strain originally called Markham, was developed in 1903. By whom?

12. The first terminal grain elevator was built by the CPR in 1883. Where was it built?

A. Winnipeg   C. Port Arthur
B. Vancouver   D. Moose Jaw

13. Saskatoon has long been known as a center of Prairie agriculture. But the first cash "crop" to leave the city was an unusual one. What was it?

A. Whisky   C. Buffalo bones
B. Buffalo droppings   D. Dried beans

14. *Paper Wheat*, the hugely successful Saskatchewan play, had as its theme a great event in Prairie agriculture. What was it?

A. The discovery that a high grade of paper could be made from discarded wheat husks.
B. The founding of Saskatchewan Wheat Pool.
C. The shipment of the first wheat crop from the port of Vancouver.
D. The great 1928 farmers' general strike.

15. In all provinces except British Columbia, Ontario, and Newfoundland, farmers and farm laborers are excluded from labor standards legislation. True or false?

16. Ontario is the only province where it is mandatory for farm employers to register under the workers' compensation scheme and pay the required premiums. True or false?

17. A farmer cannot be charged if his cattle are found on a provincial highway. True or false?

6. Symbology

Reproduced below is the Canadian Forces Badge, which is worn by servicemen and servicewomen in the Canadian Armed Forces. Lost in the black-and-white reproduction is the range of colors — blue oval shield, red maple leaves, white sword-blades and trim on crown, gold crown with multicolored gems. Here are some questions on the symbology of the Canadian Forces Badge.

1. The Crown is emblematic of what?
2. The wreath of stylized maple leaves symbolizes what?
3. The anchor, the swords, and the eagle represent what?
4. The oval shield is blue, and that color suggests what?

7. Canadian Armed Forces

Here is a barrage of questions about the Canadian Armed Forces in the recent past and present. "Canada is an unmilitary community," observed C.P. Stacey, the historian. "Warlike her people have often been forced to be; military they have never been."

1. What world "first" came about in Canada on 1 February 1968?
2. What was the Canadian Army called before 1940?
3. During the Second World War, the Royal Canadian Navy commissioned ships in various categories. One category was divided into classes called "Flower" and "Castle." What type of ship was found in this category.
4. What is the motto of the Royal Canadian Air Force?
5. In the 1940s and 1950s, highschool students could join the COTC. What did the initials stand for?
6. What is the title of the head of the Canadian Armed Forces, and to which ministry does the head report?
7. In the CAF Field Formations, which is larger, a Brigade or a Regiment? In CAF Field Formations, which is smaller, Wings or Squadrons. In CAF Naval Formations, are the following designations in decreasing order of size: Fleet, Squadrons, Ships?
8. Which Command — that is, army, navy, or air force — is equipped with each of the following?
   A. Argus.   D. Sea King.
   B. Centurion. E. Starfighter.
   C. Leopard.
9. In which city in West Germany will be found Canada's contribution to NATO forces? It is called Canadian Forces Europe.
10. Canadian Forces Base Esquimalt, on the West Coast, began as a Royal Naval hospital and depot in 1857. What is the comparable Canadian Forces Base on the East Coast, begun as a U.S. Navy base in 1918, and in what province is it found?
11. Canada has three tri-service cadet colleges. The oldest is in Kingston, Ont. Where are the other two located?
12. In the 1950s and 1960s, before the launching of satellites, Canada relied on three "lines" of warning stations — the DEW (Distant Early Warning) Line, the Mid-Canada Line, and the Pine Tree Line. To which Parallel of Latitude did each belong?
    A. 49th Parallel.
    B. 55th Parallel.
    C. 70th Parallel.
13. The Air Command has an elite squadron, named after a popular song, which specializes in demonstrating close maneuvers. What is the name of this aerobatic team?
14. What was Camp X? (Clue: It was the site of Station M — for Magic — during the Second World War.)
15. Since 1956, Canadians have seen their Armed Forces as having an international role to play in different parts of the world. What happened in 1956 to bring this about, and what is the nature of the role?

ARTS AND CRAFTS

8. Popular Paintings

From time to time the public's eye is caught by a particular painting. This
may happen more for reasons of sentimentality than for reasons of quality
— although this observation is not necessarily true for the canvases
described below. Match up the description with the once-popular painting.

1. W. Blair Bruce's scene depicting two figures in a snowstorm.
2. Ken Danby's realistic painting of a mysteriously masked goalkeeper.
3. Cornelius Krieghoff's panorama of horses and people in wild array.
4. Jean-Paul Lemieux's cutaway view of a church and its congregation.
5. David Milne's arrangement of artist's materials before a landscape.
6. Lucius R. O'Brien's breathtaking view of great cliffs.
7. Paul Peel's depiction of the backsides of two naked children.

A. "Lazarus."
B. "Painting Place."
C. "Sunrise on the Saguenay."
D. "After the Bath."
E. "The Phantom Hunter."
F. "Merrymaking."
G. "At the Crease."

9. Group of Seven

Artists are known to band together for moral support and for joint
exhibitions of their work. From 1920 on there was one supergroup, and that
was the Group of Seven. This group of painters, over the years, numbered
not seven but ten gentlemen. The names of eleven painters are given below.
Eliminate those painters who were not original members of the Group of
Seven. Name the painter who never belonged to the group.

1. Franklin Carmichael.
2. A.J. Casson.
3. Lionel LeMoine Fitzgerald.
4. Lawren Harris.
5. Edwin H. Holgate.
6. A.Y. Jackson.
7. Franz Johnston.
8. Arthur Lismer.
9. J.E.H. MacDonald.
10. Tom Thomson.
11. F.H. Varley.

---

10. Arts and Crafts

1. What is the name of the artist who in 1968 created the well-known quilt (actually a large wall-hanging which measures 244 cm (96") high and 274 cm (108") wide) that is decorated with hearts along the edge and, in block letters in the center, the words of Prime Minister Trudeau: *La Raison avant la Passion?*

2. "Jack Pine" was not a member of the Group of Seven but the title of an oil painting executed in 1916-17 by Tom _____.

3. Ronald Bloor, Arthur McKay, Ted Godwin, Douglas Morton, and Kenneth Lochhead are five artists who once lived in Regina and met at Emma Lake, Sask., where they were influenced by Barnett Newman. What was their group called?

4. Canada's leading medallist is a Hungarian-born woman with the imposing name: Dora de Pedery _____.

5. The powerful image of a horse and a train on collision course was painted in the 1950s by the realist Alex _____.

6. "Nailies" are a form of sculpture — configurations of nails in a block of wood — associated with David _____.

7. A group of Toronto artists who exhibited their abstract expressionistic works together between 1954 and 1959 included William Ronald, Harold Town, and Jack Bush. What was this group of painters called?

8. *Fraktur* is an art or craft once practiced by the Pennsylvania Dutch in places like Waterloo County, Ont. What is *Fraktur?*

9. Paul-Emile Borduas was dismissed from his teaching post at the Ecole du Meuble in Montreal in 1948 for writing a manifesto. It was called _____.

10. Carl Ray, Benjamin Chee Chee, and other Woodland Indian artists credit an older artist with being the first to tap traditional native imagery for the purposes of painting. Who is that artist?

11. Mary and Christopher _____ are highly regarded painters whose finest work deals with subject-matter found in their native province of _____.

12. The famous statue of Evangeline at Grand Pré was designed by one Hébert and completed by another Hébert. They were father and son. But was Louis-Philippe the father, and Louis-Henri the son, or *vice versa?*

13. The Saskatchewan sculptor Joe Fafard has gained a wide following for his figurines. They take the form of barnyard animals. What animal is most popular and characteristic of his work?

14. Claude Lévi-Strauss said: "I consider that the culture of the _____ produced an art on a par with that of Greece or Egypt."
15. The strongest single influence on the print-making of the Inuit came from another country. Which country?
16. Michael Snow created an appealing and graceful image that could be applied to painting, sculpture, decoration, etc. It was called "Walking _____."

---

11. Comic Art

1. Although Walt Disney, the creator of Donald Duck and Mickey Mouse, was not a Canadian, he has a connection with this country. What is it?

2. Dixon of the Mounted, The Penguin, Thunderfist, Johnny Canuck, and Nelvana of the Northern Lights were all characters found in the *Canadian Whites*. The *Canadian Whites* were:
   A. Animated short feature films in black and white made in Canada during the silent era.
   B. Comic books produced in black and white in Canada during the Second World War.
   C. Comic strips published in the *Star Weekly* during the 1940s in black and white.
   D. Comic books that bore the Good Housekeeping Seal of Approval.

3. Hal Foster was born in Halifax and made a name for himself in 1937 by writing and drawing one of the most widely admired comic strips of all time. The strip was set in the Middle Ages and was called _____.

4. Superman made his first appearance in *Action Comics*, No. 1, June 1938. He was created by Joe Shuster and Jerry Siegel who were twenty-four years old at the time. Shuster was born in Toronto, Siegel in Cleveland.
   A. Who drew the pictures? Who wrote the stories?
   B. Clark Kent, Superman's alter ego, was a reporter for the *Daily Planet*. What paper was the *Daily Planet* modelled on?
   C. What is the name of Superman's home planet?

5. Joseph Medill Patterson, the Canadian-born head of the Chicago Tribune Syndicate, purchased a comic strip about a hard-hitting police detective. The strip was called "Plainclothes Tracy" and the cartoonist was Chester Gould. Patterson changed the name of the strip. What did he call it?

6. Around the turn of the century, Palmer Cox of Granby, Que., was one of the world's most successful illustrators and cartoonists for children. He specialized in drawing little beings with pot bellies and skinny legs. What did he call these immensely popular imaginary little sprites? (A clue: The sprites delight in harmless pranks and helpful deeds and their name suggests a color.)

7. This cartoonist has a Cockney accent, an appealing manner, and an internationally syndicated cartoon called "The Outcasts." Here his name is scrambled. Unscramble it.
   W.B. SICKEN

8. There is a well-known caricature showing René Lévesque, the evening of the Parti Québécois victory, cautioning everybody: "Okay, everybody, take a Valium." The caricature was drawn by Terry Mosher but it is not signed with his name. How is it signed?

9. Match the cartoonist with his creation:
   A. Arch Dale.   i.   "Doug Wright's Family."
   B. James Simpkins.   ii. "The Doo Dads."
   C. Doug Wright.   iii. "Jasper."

---

12. Photography

There is no question that photography is an art. It is also a craft and a trade. This set of questions focuses on some of the high points in Canadian photographic life.

1. This nineteenth-century portrait photographer was widely known for his portraits of famous people. He specialized in composites — groupings of people not all of whom were present at one shooting. He had studios in Montreal, Ottawa, Halifax, Toronto, New York, Boston, Albany, and elsewhere. He was _____.

2. A powerful portrait associated with the Second World War was taken in the House of Commons on 30 December 1941. It shows a defiant Winston Churchill, and the photographer, who was relatively unknown at the time, claims the defiant scowl resulted when he removed the cigar from Churchill's mouth. The photographer's name is _____.

3. One photographer on assignment in the Barren Lands was appalled to realize that the isolated Inuit community whose lifestyle he had come to photograph for posterity was on the verge of starvation. The entire band was at death's door, and the portraits he hurriedly took and exhibited in the outside world were responsible for a relief effort that saved the lives of those who had not already died. The photographer with this unique mission is _____.

4. He was born and raised on the Prairies and trained as an abstract painter before turning to the camera. From his Tiber-side apartment in Rome, he has photographed the ruins of ancient civilizations and the glories of present ones, including Canada and Iran. There is an international public for his lavish "coffee-table books." He is _____.

5. Canada's presentation to the United States on its Bicentennary was no ordinary book, but an impressive volume of photographs. Carefully selected and beautifully reproduced, the photographs featured the border common to the two countries. The whole package was assembled by Lorraine Monk, and she called the volume _____.

6. This photographer, many maintain, has the widest following of any photographer in the country. His influence is felt through his teaching of the art at his school in rural New Brunswick, but also through his own color photographs and such books as *Photography for the Joy of It*. He once wrote a thesis on "Still Photography as a Medium of Religious Expression." His name is _____.

AWARDS & HONORS

13. Winners All!

Lucky you! You took part in a competition, or you made an outstanding
contribution in an important field. You excelled and you are being rewarded.
Which of the three alternatives best defines you or your field of endeavor?

1. If you won the Peter Jackson Trophy, you would be:
 A. A top jockey.
 B. A leading golfer.
 C. An outstanding goalkeeper.

2. If you were awarded the Tyrrell Medal, you would be:
 A. An explorer.
 B. A geologist.
 C. An historian.

3. If you received a Bessy, you would be:
 A. The composer of the most popular song of the year;
 B. The producer of the year's best TV commercial;
 C. The year's champion milk producer.

4. If you are handed a Genie, you are:
 A. In the record business.
 B. In the film industry.
 C. In the fashion world.

5. If you accept a Charlie or a Dan, you are:
 A. A newspaper reporter.
 B. A radio or television reporter.
 C. A broadcast news editor.

6. If you earned the Minto Cup, you were successful in:
   A. Badminton.
   B. Hockey.
   C. Lacrosse.
7. If you won the Macdonald Briar, you were tops for the year in:
   A. Archery.
   B. Curling.
   C. Lacrosse.
8. If you accepted a Juno, it means that you are busy:
   A. As a broadcaster.
   B. As a recording artist.
   C. As a theater person.
9. If you are chosen to receive the Herzberg Medal, it means you are:
   A. A physicist.
   B. A philanthropist.
   C. A physician.
10. If you earned the Vézina Trophy, you are:
    A. The outstanding offensive or defensive player.
    B. The goalkeeper with fewest goals scored against him.
    C. The most popular sports personality of the year.
11. If you accept the Earle Grey Award, you are:
    A. A television actor or actress.
    B. A television producer.
    C. A television playwright.
12. If you are deemed worthy of the Dora, you are:
    A. A television personality.
    B. A radio personality.
    C. A stage personality.
13. If you received the Massey Medal you are a geographer, but if you received a Massey Award you are:
    A. A distinguished architect.
    B. An outstanding artist.
    C. A world statesman.
14. If you are selected to receive one of the Gairdner Foundation International Awards, it means you have contributed to:
    A. The cause of world peace.
    B. The sum of scientific knowledge.
    C. The relief of human suffering.

---

14. Nobel Laureates

Since 1901 the Nobel Prizes have been awarded for achievement in different fields of endeavor. Among the Nobel laureates there are a number of Canadians. There is no reason not to take national pride in the distinguished achievements of these laureates, whatever their stripe — citizens, former citizens, new citizens, etc. In addition, some prizes have gone for work done in Canada. Do you deserve a Nobel Prize for your knowledge of Canadian Nobel Prize laureates? Find out!

1. Is the following statement true of false? Dr. Frederick Grant Banting and Professor J.J.R. Macleod jointly received the prize for Medicine for the isolation of Insulin.

2. When he accepted the prize for Peace in 1957, who said: "The grim fact is that we prepare for war like precocious giants and for peace like retarded pygmies"?

3. Dr. Gerhard Herzberg of the National Research Council received the prize in Chemistry in 1971 for:
   A. Experiments in the biosynthesis of carbohydrates.
   B. Theory of plasma physics.
   C. Studies in Spectroscopy.

4. Is the following sentence right or wrong? Dr. William F. Giauque (Chemistry, 1949) and Dr. Charles B. Huggins (Medicine, 1966) are two naturalized American Nobel laureates who were born in Canada.

5. Saul Bellow, the novelist, is the first Canadian citizen to receive the Nobel Prize for Literature. True or false.

6. Guglielmo Marconi received the prize in Physics in 1909 (jointly with Ferdinand Braun). What is the Italian inventor's Canadian connection?

7. Two scientists conducted experiments at the Macdonald Physics Laboratory at McGill University between 1898 and 1907 and later received Nobel Prizes in Chemistry. Who were they?

8. Does Har Gobind Khorana, a native of India, who shared the prize in Medicine with others in 1968, have a Canadian connection? Yes or no.

BUILDINGS

15. Residences of Renown

Important people live in stately homes — in the past, anyway, when ostentation was an important aspect of public life. On the left appear the names of twenty-one stately homes; on the right appear the names of past, present, or official occupants. Match them up before moving day!

1. Batterwood.
2. Casa Loma.
3. Château de Ramezay.
4. Château St. Louis.
5. Chiefswood.
6. Chorley Park.
7. Clifton.
8. Dundurn.
9. Dunsmuir.
10. Earnscliffe.
11. Glensmere.
12. Headley.
13. Laurier House.
14. Malahide.
15. Parkwood.
16. Ravenscrag.
17. Rideau Hall.
18. Spencer Wood
19. Stornoway.
20. 24 Sussex Drive.
21. Uniak House.

A. Pierre Elliott Trudeau.
B. Richard John Uniak.
C. Joe Clark and Maureen McTeer.
D. Edward Schreyer.
E. Sir Adam Beck.
F. W.L. Mackenzie King.
G. Thomas Talbot.
H. Samuel de Champlain.
I. Vincent Massey.
J. Sir Allan Napier McNab.
K. Sir Henry Pellatt.
L. Sir John A. Macdonald.
M. Lord Monck.
N. Robert Borden.
O. Joseph Brant.
P. Claude de Ramezay.
Q. Sir James Dunsmuir.
R. Sir Hugh Allan.
S. Samuel L. McLaughlin.
T. Thomas Chandler Haliburton.
U. George F. Ferguson.

16. Chateaux in Canada

To have a castle in Spain is to have an ideal or an illusion, but to have a chateau in Canada is to possess something substantial. Answer the following questions about these chateaux.

1. The Château Clique is not a place to stay. What was it?
2. The Château de Ramezay is not a hotel but a _____ in Montreal.
3. The Château Frontenac, the most imposing and historic of the CP hotels, is located on a promontory overlooking _____.
4. Château Gai is no happy motel. Instead, it is the name of an Ontario _____.
5. Château Lake Louise is a beautifully sited railway hotel overlooking Lake Louise in Alberta. Is it owned by the CN or CP?
6. The Château Laurier is a CN hotel located in _____.
7. The Château Montebello is a favorite resort hotel located in Quebec. It is owned by the CN or CP. Which?
8. Château St. Louis, no longer standing, was the official residence in Quebec City of _____.
9. Châteauguay, southwest of _____, was the site of an important battle in the War of 1812.

---

17. What Building Is This?

Of the notable buildings across the country, here is a selection. Identify the structure and the province in which it is located.

1.

2.

3.

4.

5.

6.

7.

8.

9.

10.

11.

12.

13.

18. Architects All

There are many notable buildings to be found across the country, but few great ones. This quiz draws attention to some memorable structures and their architects. Once seen, these buildings are seldom forgotten. The names of their designers are often less familiar. Match up the architect with the work of art.

1. Casa Loma, Toronto.
2. Château Frontenac, Quebec City.
3. Empress Hotel, Victoria.
4. Habitat, Montreal.
5. Massey College, Toronto.
6. Metropolitan Toronto Library, Toronto.
7. Museum of Anthropology, Vancouver.
8. National Arts Centre, Ottawa.
9. New City Hall, Toronto.
10. Parliament Buildings, Ottawa.
11. Province House, Halifax.
12. Place Bonaventure, Montreal.
13. Place Ville Marie, Montreal.
14. Simon Fraser University, Burnaby, B.C.
15. University College, Toronto.

A. Raymond Affleck.
B. Charles Baillarge, Thomas Fuller, and J.A. Pearson.
C. F.W. Cumberland.
D. Arthur Erickson.
E. Arthur Erickson.
F. Fred Lebensold.
G. E.J. Lennox.
H. Raymond Moriyama.
I. I.M. Pei.
J. Bruce Price.
K. F.M. Rattenbury.
L. Viljo Revell.
M. Moshe Safdie.
N. Richard Scott.
O. Ron Thom.

19. Memorable Memorials

There are not all that many statues to distinguished people erected in our cities, but some of the memorials that have been raised are memorable.

1. In which city does there stand, somewhat stiffly, the life-like statue of the saloon-keeper John "Gassy Jack" Deighton?
2. In which city does there rise above a park and a beach the rugged, larger-than-life likeness of Samuel de Champlain?
3. In which city must one look to the dome of the Legislative Building to spy the thirteen-foot gilded bronze figure of a youth, a torch in his right hand, a sheaf of wheat in his left?
4. In which city is there a romantic statue of the brave knight Sir Galahad, erected to commemorate a young man who drowned in a vain attempt to rescue a little girl who had been skating?
5. In which city will one be surprised to see an oversized fibreglass effigy of Professor Josiah Flintabbaty Flonatin, a character out of a dime novel?

20. Misnomers

Here are some mistakes, or misnomers, to correct. Those unfamiliar with our country might say, "So what's wrong?" But a Canadian, familiar with the phraseology and facts of life in this country, will say, "That's wrong!"

1. Peace, order, and the pursuit of happiness.
2. Nine provinces against two.
3. The Baby Premium.
4. The British North American Act.
5. Polyculturalism and dual lingualism.
6. The Canadian Council of the Arts, Humanities, and Social Sciences.
7. Three northern territories.
8. North of Sixty-five.
9. Daylight Spending Time.
10. Trail of '88.
11. The twenty-first century belongs to Canada.
12. Forty-eighth Parallel.
13. Western Standard Time.
14. Apprehended resurrection.
15. The three Atlantic Provinces.
16. The three Western Provinces.
17. The Father of Confederation.

21. Fun With Words

Here are some peculiarities of the English language which are of particular interest to Canadians, for they turn on words or phrases that are associated with this country. How many of these questions about linguistic oddities are you able to answer?

1. A palindrome is a word or phrase that reads the same backwards or forwards. NIAGARA, O ROAR AGAIN! is a palindrome. The name of a leading Canadian university is a palindrome. What is it?

2. An anagram is a word or phrase the letters of which may be rearranged to create another word or phrase. The word ANAGRAMS may be changed into ARS MAGNA (Latin for "great art").
   A. REAL SAP GUM is an anagram of a two-word foodstuff exported widely. What are those two words?
   B. MA BELL RANG, ALEX HEARD is an anagrammatical form of the name of an inventor associated with Canada. Who is the inventor?
   C. SOME SKI is a rearrangement of the letters that form the name of a native group. Which group?
   D. TWO CANADIAN PROVINCES: LANDS I DREAD! This amusing phrase disguises, in anagrammatical form, the names of two provinces connected by the word "and." What provinces? (Clue: One of the provinces has three words in its name.)

3. An acronym is a word formed of the initial letters of other words. HOMES is an acronym for the names of some bodies of water. If you remember the names of the bodies of water, HOMES is also a mnemonic. Is it a mnemonic for you?

4. Although there are no major centers with the name Adanac, there are a number of small businesses with this name in the country. Why is Adanac considered a patriotic and particularly appropriate name in this country?

---

22. The Force

The Royal Canadian Mounted Police is among the most important and most recognized institutions inside and outside the country. The RCMP has a long and quite honorable history, dating back to 1873 when it was created as a civilian police force to patrol the West. These questions based on the history of the Force should be a "snap" to answer.

1. It was not always called the Royal Canadian Mounted Police. What was the Force originally called when it was created in May 1873?

2. The original name of the Force was changed in 1904, when it was honored by the King of England. What new name was it given?

3. The present name came into existence in 1920 when the Force took over the policing duties of the old Dominion Police. Today the RCMP, as well as acting as the federal police force, does duty as the provincial police force in both Territories and in all but two of the provinces. Which provinces have their own Provincial Police?

4. "They Always Get Their Man" is not the official motto of the Force. The official motto is _____.

5. The head of the RCMP is known as the:
   A. Commander.   C. Director-General.
   B. Commissioner.   D. Inspector-General.

6. The RCMP has many nicknames, including "The Mounties," "The Horsemen," and "The Force." The origin of these is obvious, but why has the RCMP been called "The Barnburners"?

7. The initials of the RCMP in French are GRC. Can you expand and explain what these letters stand for?

8. Red uniforms were chosen over blue — the customary color for police garb — to suggest to the population of the West that the new Force would uphold the law as did the British Army (which wore red coats). Explain the meaning of the following:
   A. Red Serge.
   B. Scarlet and Stetson.
9. The Mountie is a familiar figure in comic books, in the movies, and on television. But who is that famous Mountie, Sergeant Renfrew (and his dog Cuddles)?

---

23. Innumerable Numbers

Here is a numbers game that is perfectly legal. A specific Canadian meaning attaches to each of these numerical expressions. Without consulting a reference work, how many are you able to identify?

1. No. 1 Manitoba Hard.
2. Two Solitudes.
3. Three-Pence Beaver.
4. Four-Minute Mile.
5. 5BX.
6. Six Nations.
7. Seven Oaks.
8. Eight Men Speak.
9. Nine-Hour Day.
10. Ten Lost Years.
11. Twelve-Foot Davis.
12. The Seventeen.
13. Thirty Acres.
14. 92 Resolutions.
15. Trail of '98.
16. One Hundred Associates
17. The 401.
18. 1837-1937.
19. 30,000 Islands.
20. One Million Children.
21. Last Post Fund.

CORPORATIONS

24. Capitalists

"One of the great problems before Canada today is not to save capitalism from socialism or communism, but to save capitalism from certain capitalists." This opinion was expressed by Grattan O'Leary to members of the Empire Club in 1933. O'Leary's opinion has no necessary relationship with the following gentlemen, capitalists all, who are identified by the general public with a corporation, an industry, or a line of products and services. Match up the corporate head with the company or concern.

1. Thomas J. Bata.		A.	Hockey, Auto Sales, and Real Estate Development.
2. Conrad Black.		B.	Publishing and sports.
3. S. Robert Blair.		C.	Newspaper holdings.
4. Charles Bronfman.		D.	Dome Petroleum Ltd.
5. Robert Campeau.		E.	Lumber, smelting, publishing.
6. Jack Kent Cooke.		F.	Power Corporation of Canada.
7. Paul Desmarais.		G.	Biscuits, tea, etc.
8. A. Ephraim Diamond		H.	Harlequin Books.
9. Peter Pocklington.		I.	Iron ore.
10. The Eaton Bros.		J.	Scotch whiskey.
11. J. Patrick Gallagher.		K.	Alberta Gas Trunk Pipeline.
12. Beland Honderich.		L.	Brascan Ltd.
13. K.C. Irving.		M.	Argus Corporation.
14. John H. Moore.		N.	Construction.
15. Brian Mulroney.		O.	Cadillac Fairview Corporation.
16. The reichmann Bros.		P.	Uranium.
17. Stephen B. Roman.		Q.	Retailers.
18. Ian Sinclair.		R.	Developers.
19. Kenneth Thomson.		S.	Canadian Pacific Ltd.
20. Galen Weston.		T.	Shoes.

25. Corporate Identities

"I hold no brief for private enterprise," noted C.L. Burton, long-time chairman of the Robert Simpson Company in 1952. "But I have unshakeable faith in individual enterprise." Here are some questions about individual enterprises of which the public is already aware.

1. What company, founded in 1942, has registered the following trade names — Ski-Doo and Moto-Ski for snowmobiles, LRC for trains, and Can-Am for motorcycles?
2. Here are some household names — McCormick's Biscuits, Neilson's Chocolate, Donlands Dairy, National Tea Co., White Swan Company, E.B. Eddy Forest Products Ltd. What equally well-known company owns and operates these companies? It goes back to 1882.
3. "They Wear Longer Because They're Made Stronger" . . . "Work and Casual Wear for the Whole Family" . . . "Anything Goes" . . . "Fit Where It Counts" . . . "Buckskin Cotton Denims" . . . "Nev'r Press" . . . "Bum Bum." These are slogans and trade names associated with which manufacturing company?
4. What is the present-day name of a large chemical company that was founded in Hamilton in 1862 and has changed its name a number of times, one change being from CXL (for Canadian Explosives Limited)?
5. What does Téléglobe Canada do?
6. What is the largest Canadian-owned company in the petroleum business?
7. Identify the speaker who told an interviewer in 1975: "I just followed the same business principles that worked in Timmins and North Bay. I did the same things in Edinburgh and London as I did back here, except I added a few zeros at the end." (Clue: He founded one of Canada's hundred largest companies.)
8. Once, when someone suggested Canada was an underdeveloped country, he quipped, "If Canada is underdeveloped, so is Brigitte Bardot." Who made this remark? (Clue: He was a founder of the country's largest forest-products operation.)

26. Inspired Commercials

The lines that follow, backed by music and visuals on television, or by beguiling artwork in newspapers and magazines, should be familiar to millions of Canadians. But divorced from the products they are promoting, do they bring back the sponsor's or manufacturer's name? These are top-of-the-line commercials, slogans, campaigns, or guarantees. Identify them.

1. At Speedy You're a Somebody.
2. Good Sports.
3. Goods Satisfactory or Money Refunded.
4. Hey Mabel, Black Label!
5. It's Mainly because of the Meat!
6. More than the Price is Right.
7. Only in Canada . . . Pity.
8. Our Product is Steel. Our Strength is People.
9. Sanitation for the Nation.
10. Thank you very much, Milk.

EDUCATION

27. Higher Learning

"A little learning is a dangerous thing," wrote Bob Edwards, publisher of the Calgary *Eye Opener*, "but a lot of ignorance is just as bad." Here are some institutions of higher learning — universities. Match them with their sites.

1. Acadia University.
2. Athabasca University.
3. Bishop's University.
4. Carleton University.
5. Concordia University.
6. Dalhousie University.
7. Laval University.
8. McMaster University.
9. Memorial University.
10. Mount Allison University.
11. Queen's University.
12. St. Francis Xavier University.
13. Simon Fraser University.
14. Trent University.
15. University of Western Ontario.
16. Wilfrid Laurier University.
17. York University.

A. Ottawa, Ont.
B. Sackville, N.B.
C. Quebec City, Que.
D. Kingston, Ont.
E. Edmonton, Alta.
F. Antigonish, N.S.
G. Burnaby, B.C.
H. London, Ont.
I. Waterloo, Ont.
J. Toronto, Ont.
K. Peterborough, Ont.
L. Wolfville, N.S.
M. Montreal, Que.
N. Lennoxville, Que.
O. St. John's, Nfld.
P. Hamilton, Ont.
Q. Halifax, N.S.

28. Worlds of Learning

This set of questions has been designed to show that there is not one single world of learning but many worlds of learning. Not all instruction or

education takes place in the classroom; indeed, most of it takes place in the "real world," as some of these movements and developments show.

1. What is the name of the internationally known movement designed to make men and women "masters of their own destiny"? The movement, which stressed co-operative self-help, grew out of an extension program at St. Francis Xavier University in Nova Scotia.

2. There is a volunteer group that through correspondence courses and field teachers provides educational opportunities for workers in isolated mining, lumber, and railway camps. During the summer, college students work at these sites by day and offer free instruction in the evening. Name the organization.

3. In 1927, a priest arrived in Wilcox, Sask., with fifteen boys. Six years later, in the depth of the Depression, with no campus, no experience, and no money, he actually founded a college to help young people of the poverty-stricken prairies acquire higher education. The students were called The Hounds. What was the college, and who was its ebullient founder?

4. It began with the national office of the YMCA offering academic and vocational instruction to members of the Canadian Armed Forces in 1917-19, an it was revived for the period 1945-46. It offered junior college and extension service and it took its name from the dust-colored uniforms worn by soldiers. What was it called?

5. This organization supplied "cultural uplift" to those who lived in rural communities and small towns across Canada. It was mainly active in this country on the prairies from 1915 to 1935. It traveled from site to site, setting up its tents, and presenting as many as a dozen different shows each day for up to six days — lectures, demonstrations, presentations, talks, concerts, etc. Name the organization.

6. Founded in 1961, one year before the U.S. Peace Corps, it is a volunteer service for young Canadians in developing countries. It is funded by the Canadian International Development Agency, by universities, and by interested individuals and organizations. It provides skilled volunteers to countries and communities which are eager for their services. Name the group.

7. The Canadian Broadcasting Corporation and the Canadian Association for Adult Education joined forces to offer radio listeners a series of self-help programs. Heard from 1939 to 1960, the series encouraged rural audiences to gather in small groups in neighbors' homes to (in the words of the program) "read — listen — discuss — act" on its information. What was the series called?

8. Located near Victoria, B.C. and opened in September 1974, this secondary school is the third in a world-wide series of United World Colleges dedicated to promoting international understanding and fellowship. Half of the students are Canadian, the rest from other countries. Name the school.

FAUNA AND FLORA

29. Mammal-Watching

Mammals are animals that suckle their young. The class excludes fish but includes marine species like whales; it excludes birds but includes aerial species like bats. There are over four hundred species of mammals in the world, and many are found in Canada. Answer the following questions based on mammals described and depicted by William Henry Burt in *A Field Guide to the Mammals* (3d ed., 1976).

1. The Arctic shrew is the most brilliant colored and attractive member of the shrew family. True or false.
2. The largest living carnivores, or meat-eaters, are the bears, with head and body ranging from five to eight feet in height. Which is the tallest — the black bear, the grizzly bear, the Alaskan brown bear, or the polar bear?
3. The wolverine, which has been called one of the few remnants of true wilderness, looks like a small bear and ranges across the North and in British Columbia. True or false.
4. Does the gray wolf, the largest of the wild dogs, run with its tail carried high or low?
5. A true scavenger, the Arctic _____ follows the Polar Bear in winter and feasts on the scraps it leaves behind. Fill in the blank.
6. The walrus lives on ice flows and islands in the Arctic. It is a large mammal. Which of the following *two* statements are true?
   A. The male is 2.4 m (8') high, the female 1.8 m (6') high.
   B. The male weighs 1225.5 kg (2,700 lbs), the female 816.7 kg (1,800 lbs).
   C. The male is 3.6 m (12') high, the female 2.7 m (9') high.
   D. The male weighs 952.8 kg (2,100 lbs), the female 544.5 kg (1,200 lbs).
   E. The male and female are approximately 2.7 m (9') high.
   F. The male and female are approximately 907 kg (2,000 lbs) apiece.
7. Inuit hunt the Arctic ground squirrel for food and fur. This large squirrel

hibernates for seven months of the year. It has a gestation period of twenty-five days and grows rapidly. True or false.

8. Whatever is a little brown myotis?

9. What is another name for *Castor canadensis?*

10. Canada has no shortage of lemmings, small vole-like mammals popularly believed to harbor the death wish. But which one of the following is a non-existent lemming?

   A. Brown lemming.
   B. Gray lemming.
   C. Greenland collared lemming.
   D. Hudson Bay collared lemming.
   E. Northern bog lemming.
   F. Southern bog lemming.

11. The Arctic hare occupies the Barren Lands and the slightly smaller Snowshoe hare occupies plains or boreal forests. Or is it the other way round?

12. The moose is distinguished from other animals by its great size, its overhanging snout, its pendant "bell" on its throat, and its ungainly appearance. True or false.

13. Is it truthful to say that the woodland caribou and the barren-ground caribou are both excellent game mammals?

14. Unlike the bison, the mountain goat, and the bighorn sheep, to which it is related, the muskox of the Far North is the only member of the bovid family with long, silky, brown hair that hangs shirtlike nearly to its feet. True or false.

15. The white whale is actually pale green in color. True or false.

16. Give the popular name of the *Monodon monoceros,* which has a long, spirally twisted "unicorn" tusk projecting forward from its blunt snout.

---

30. Flower-Watching

There are some six thousand species of flora, or plant life, in Canada. Among the most pleasing of these species are the wildflowers which grow in such profusion in the varied habitats of the country: in woodlands; in fields and meadows; in arctic and alpine regions; and in marshes and bogs. Some common wildflowers — reproduced in full color in *Canadian Wildflowers* (1976) by Mary Ferguson and Richard M. Saunders — are described in these multiple-choice questions.

1. This lovely flower found in the Eastern Woodlands is a native North American species. It has a striking appearance. The large white flower has three petals and three leaves. As it ages the petals turn pink and sometimes deep magenta. It is called:

   A. Cut-leaved Toothwort.
   B. Diapensia.
   C. Great White Trillium.

2. Here is another woodland flower. It grows in partial shade and is usually described as stemless (though it rises to a height of 38 cm or 15"). The

predominant color is pink, from pale to deep. The flower resembles an upside-down, semi-inflated balloon. Its name is:

A. Moccasin Flower.

B. Partridge Berry.

C. Red or Pink Monkey Flower.

3. Because at blooms before the snow has melted from the prairies or meadows, this brave little flower has been called "the harbinger of spring." It is pale to deep mauve in color and it gives the prairie a smoky appearance. It protects itself with tiny hairs on its stem, leaves, and sepals. It was named after the Greek word for wind. It is known as:

A. Common Thistle.

B. Prairie Crocus.

C. Teasel.

4. Another meadow plant, this one is so plain (although pleasant in its own way) that it is taken for granted. It was introduced by colonists, and it looks like a yellow sun surrounded by a blaze of thin white petals. Lovers pull these leaves and recite "She loves me, she loves me not" until they are all gone. Its name could only be:

A. Cloudberry.

B. Ox-eye Daisy.

C. Starry Chickweed.

5. This alpine or arctic flower has large leaves, silvery in color, with inconspicuous, pale, yellow-lined silver flowers on the axils of the leaves. Its berries are edible though very dry. It grows on dry slopes along streams and lakesides and rises in height from 61 cm to 3.7 m (2 to 12 ft). This aromatic wildflower is called:

A. Bear Grass.

B. Mountain Phacelia.

C. Wolf Willow.

6. Also an arctic or alpine flower, this one has tiny flowers that are less than 1.25 cm (a half-inch) in diameter. The plant is vivid when growing on mountains, for it forms a two-inch mat and clings to rock or gravelly places. When it blooms, from June to August, it is bright pink in color. Its name is:

A. Lapland Rosebay.

B. Moss Campion.

C. Purple Mountain Saxifrage.

7. Here is a flower that seems to float serenely on quiet water. Its many-petalled bowls make it a most elegant ornament. The white flower measures from 2.5 to 10 cm (one to four inches) across, and it rides among pads that are green on top and purple underneath. It is perfumed, as well, and is of the same genus as the lotus. Call it:

A. Canada Anemone.

B. Fragrant White Water Lily.

C. Water Arum.

8. Another flower of marshes and bogs is one that produces umbrella-like flowers which are purple, wine-red, or yellow-green. The flowers grow on stems from 30.5 to 50.8 cm (twelve to twenty inches) high. Insects are

caught in its hollow leaves, drowned in its watery liquid, and then digested. This carnivorous plant is known as:

A. Jack-in-the-Pulpit.

B. Pitcher Plant.

C. Snapdragon.

---

31. Bird-Watching

Over five hundred species of birds have been observed in Canada. Photographers enjoy taking their pictures; sportsmen relish shooting them; taxidermists find pleasure in mounting them; chefs are challenged to cook them; artists strive to paint them; ornithologists delight in classifying them; and naturalists take pride in spotting and identifying them, often with handbooks like Stuart L. Thompson's *160 Birds to Know* (1970). Here are some characteristics of ten birds that are familiar pretty well across the country. How many can you identify?

1. White plumage, yellow heads, head without "horns," feet feathered to the toes. No ear tufts. No other Canadian bird of prey is so pure white, though it may appear with some dark markings. Diurnal in habits, most of the time it is found in the Far North. Identify it.

2. A large perching bird. The entire plumage is jet-black, with bluish or purplish seen. In flight, its wing strikes the air with regularity. It has a simple sound: *caw*. This bird has a poor reputation, for it destroys the eggs and the young of small birds, uproots corn, and feasts on carrion. What is it?

3. One of the commonest of birds. It is identified by the central breast spot. This little brown bird is striped with darker brown, with the head more finely striped still. Below it is whitish, with dark brown concentric streaks tending to form a spot in the center of its breast. Its call is *chimp* or *chink*. It is partial to places near water. Name it.

4. Typical of the northern lake country. It is a large, goose-like bird with a sharp bill. The head is black, the neck is black but streaked with bands of white, and the back is black with many squarish white spots. It has a quivering laugh or a wolfish howl. It is an aquatic bird and the young may ride on the backs of their parents. What is it called?

5. So familiar as scarcely to require description. The head is black; the back and wings are gray; the tail is dark with white tips; the eye-ring is broken white. The tell-tale characteristic is the brick-red breast. Its call is a low *chuck*. This widely distributed bird is a familiar sight on lawns or in city parks where it is a great hunter for worms. What is its name?

6. A noisy, active bird. This is a blue-and-white bird with a prominent, bright blue crest. It has two calls: *jay, jay;* and *side-light, side-light*. It remains in winter and often visits feeding stations without fear. Identify it.

7. Stunning to look at. The male has a rich, bright-red body with jet-black face, huge bill, and prominent crest. The female is dull olive-brown with tinges of red on crest, wings, and tail. Its call is a low *tseep* or a high *whit, whee-o;* its song is *wheea-a, whee-a, whee-a*. It remains year-round. What is it?

8. A splendid game bird. This plump, chicken-like bird has mottled plumage — browns, grays, buffs, and white (in broad patches and fine lines). In winter the toes produce fringes of tiny quills to enable it to walk on snow. Often

the only glimpse one has of this bird is of a gray form disappearing in a startling whir of wings. What is it called?

9. A stately yet somewhat ungainly bird. It has a general bluish color but with a white face and crown and a black crest. Generally a glum bird, it nests in colonies. Its habitats are ponds, rivers, and shallow water. Its hoarse croak may even be heard at night. Identify it.

10. A noble bird of huge size and spectacular manner. It has a sooty-black head and neck, except for a broad white patch extending from below the bill upwards behind the eye. It sounds a long, sonorous single note *ongk*, repeated in varying pitches and sometimes doubled. It migrates in a characteristic v-shaped formation and is said to mate for life. What is its name?

---

32. Fish-Watching

Fishing supplies employment and food, not to mention pleasure, for a great many Canadians. Here is a set of questions concerned with commercial and other aspects of "the catch."

1. The Grand Banks, off the coast of the province of _____, are among the world's largest fishing grounds.
2. The principal fish of the East Coast of Canada is the _____.
3. The principal fish of the West Coast of Canada is the _____.
4. The staple fish of the Pacific fisheries comes in five important varieties. These are: S_____, C_____, S_____, P_____, and C_____.
5. Next in economic importance to the Grand Banks and the Pacific Coast fisheries are the inland fisheries. The most important of the inland fisheries are those of the _____.
6. By what declaration of the federal government did the coastal fisheries benefit on 1 January 1977?
7. Roderick Haig-Brown was a leading naturalist and angler, but yet confessed, "Perhaps fishing is for me only an excuse to be near _____."

---

33. Knock on Wood

Forests engulfed the first explorers and early settlers. Many of these trees are standing to this day, and Canadians have consistently turned to the forests of the country for their livelihood and to maintain their standard of living. How many of the following questions about our forest and its products are you able to answer correctly?

1. Fill in the blank and state whether the following sentence is true or false. "Canada has an estimated _____ of the total of the world's forests and is the world's major exporter of forest products."
   A. 7%.
   B. 17%.
   C. 27%.

2. "The forest industries comprise the most important single manufacturing sector in Canada in terms of employment, dollar value of the final product, and foreign exchange earnings." True or false.

3. Fill in the blank. "Canada is one of the world's largest manufacturers of newsprint, producing 8.8 million tonnes annually, or _____ of the total world production."
   A. 17%.
   B. 27%.
   C. 37%.
   D. 47%.

4. All the trees that are found in Canadian forests are either *coniferous* or *deciduous*.
   A. What is the meaning of *coniferous*?
   B. What is the meaning of *deciduous*?
   C. Are more native tree species coniferous or deciduous?

5. Trees found in Canadian forests are divided into two types: hardwoods and softwoods.
   A. Are hardwoods coniferous or deciduous?
   B. Are softwoods deciduous or coniferous?

6. Listed here, in alphabetical order, are six common species of trees. Three are coniferous, three are deciduous. Which are which?
   A. Douglas-fir.
   B. Yellow Birch.
   C. Jack Pine.
   D. Sitka Spruce.
   E. Sugar Maple.
   F. White oak.

7. True or false. More Douglas-fir trees ar marketed than Spruce trees.

8. Complete the following couplet written by Raymond Souster:
   ". . . But only God can make a tree."
   (He'll never try it in _____.)"

34. Banking

"When I go into a bank I get rattled," wrote Stephen Leacock in a famous essay. Here are some questions about banks, finance, and the world of money.

1. The oldest chartered bank in Canada was founded in Montreal in 1917. It now has over twelve hundred branches and offices including those in over forty foreign countries. What is it called?

2. What bank began operating in 1935 to regulate "credit and currency in the best interests of the economic life of the nation"?

3. Which is the largest chartered bank in the country?

4. The country's largest banks are called the "Big Five." Here they are, in order of size. What are their names?
   A. _____.
   B. Canadian _____ Bank of _____.
   C. Bank of _____.
   D. Bank of _____.
   E. _____ Bank.

5. Banks are federally chartered, but _____ are federally or provincially chartered.

6. The first *caisse populaire* was opened in Lévis, Que., in 1900. There are now thousands across the country. What is it in English?

7. What was the name of the chairman of the Commission on Tax Reform who said in 1967, "A buck is a buck"?

8. What is the name of the famous essay written by Stephen Leacock which deals with personal banking? It is quoted above and it appeared in his book *Literary Lapses* in 1910.

35. Coins and Stamps

Many Canadians are numismatists and philatelists — that is, they collect coins and stamps. The study is not only educational and pleasurable but also profitable, as coins and stamps are a good hedge against inflation. Here are some non-specialist questions on Canadian numismatics and philately.

1. Canada's currency is regulated by the Royal Canadian Mint. Chartered by the British Royal Mint in 1870, the Ottawa Mint opened in 1908. It became the _____ in 1931 and a _____ in 1969. It is located in Ottawa and Hull; in 1976, a branch plant was opened near _____, Man. The chief executive officer is called the _____.

2. In 1936, when Edward VIII abdicated in favor of George VI, the Mint was faced with a problem. The shortage of one-cent and ten-cent pieces could be alleviated only by the issuing of new coins. But the new dies of George VI were not ready for use; the current dies of Edward VIII could not be reused as he had abdicated; and the old dies of George V were clearly marked 1936, the year of his death. What did the Mint do?

3. Why were all denominations of banknotes issued in 1954 quickly dubbed "Devil in the Hair"?

4. British authorities established postal service at Halifax in 1755. Eight years later, _____, an American, became the first postmaster of _____. Great Britain introduced the world's first _____ postal service in 1840, and nine years later passed legislation permitting the colonial governments to establish their own postal systems. In British North America, seven local governments (including _____) proceeded to do so and to issue stamps.

5. The first stamp to appear was issued by the Province of Canada in 1851. It showed a plump _____, was orange-red in color, and sold for three _____. It was popularly called the _____. The designer was Sir _____.

6. The first commemorative appeared for Christmas 1898, and it celebrated the introduction of Imperial penny postage. It was the Dominion's first stamp in two colors (black and _____), and many complained because the _____ was out of register. This stamp bore a bold legend: "We Hold a Vaster Empire _____."

7. Whose portrait appeared on the one-cent stamp issued in 1935. Why is that stamp called the "Weeping Princess"?

8. On 1 July 1948, the Post Office Department announced its "all-up" policy. What was it?

9. The Canada Post Office introduced its new _____ in the 1970s, and it identifies eighteen geographical divisions of the country with its alphanumeric code. Now known as Canada Post, in 1982 it became a _____.

FOLKLORE

36. Name That Monster

The woods and waters of this country teem with strange beings and weird beasts. Some range widely; others haunt locally. The following monsters are nationally notorious. Are you able to identify them from the imaginary speeches that follow. Is it a being or a beast that is speaking? And what do men call it?

1. My heart is of ice, my haunt is the wild woods. When I fly, it is faster than a human's cry. I am the legendary demon of the woods who devours Indian and white alike. My name, in Algonkian, means cannibal, for I am known as
_____.

2. They call me the wild woman of the woods, and they claim I steal their children and carry them off to my cave. It is true, for all they do is stand there. My cry — "OO-oo-oo-oeo" — frightens them to the point of death. In the woods and caves I live, near the sea. Call me _____.

3. I avoid the white man as much as I may, for he wishes to shoot me with his rifle or his camera with telescopic sight. So cumbersome and hairy am I that it takes me some time to find refuge in the mountainous regions. The footprints I leave behind intrigue my pursuers, so I confuse them and double back. They will never find me for I am _____.

4. My eyes blink and lightning flashes; my beak snaps and thunder sounds. All I do is flap my wings and gale-force winds knock down the teepees and the tents. Avoid me in my habitat, in my eerie, amid the rocky peaks of the mountains. Beware the _____.

5. In the lower depths do I dwell. From my cut-off fingers did grow the seals, the walruses, and the sea mammals. The tales of me told by the Inuit are true. So they are careful lest they summon me, me, whom the spirits call
_____.

6. I avoid them like the plague, the natives and the tourists both, for they want to disturb me in my watery depths. They see me as very large, very long, very ancient, prehistoric some say. Hark, here comes a boatload of visitors

now! Watch me vanish beneath the surface of the lake. You have just spotted _____.

---

37. Folk Songs

The traditional songs of many lands are sung in Canada, but the majority of folk songs sung by Canadians come from the British Isles and France. Some are indigenously Canadian in words, in music, or in a combination of the two. Here are the lyrics — missing key words, alas! — of some moving Canadian folk songs. They should be known by everyone. The texts appear in Edith Fowke's *The Penguin Book of Canadian Folk Songs* (1973). Fill in the blanks and give the titles of these songs.

1. _____ _____ _____
   Banni de ses foyers,

   _____ _____
   Banni de ses foyers,
   Parcourait en pleurant
   Des pays étrangers,
   Parcourait en pleurant
   Des pays étrangers.

2. Hurrah for our own native isle, _____!
   Not a stranger shall hold one inch of its strand!
   Her face turns to Britain, her back to the Gulf.
   Come near at your peril, Canadian _____!

3. We'll _____ and we'll _____ like true Newfoundlanders,
   We'll rant and we'll roar on deck and below
   Until we see bottom inside the two sunkers,
   When straight through the Channel to Toslow we'll go.

4. _____ _____ _____ _____, the sea-bound coast,
   Let your mountains dark and dreary be,
   For when I am far away on the briny ocean tossed,
   Will you ever heave a sigh and a wish for me?

5. My name 'tis _____ _____, as you may understand.
   I was born on Prince Edward's Island near by the ocean strand.
   In eighteen hundred and eighty-four when the flowers were a brilliant hue,
   I left my native counterie my fortune to pursue.

6. "Maw! Maw! I want to go home to my Maw!
   This blooming country's a _____, and I want to go home to my Maw!"

7. There was birch rine, tar twine, cherry wine and turpentine,
   Jowls and cavalances, ginger beer and tea,
   Pigs' feet, cats' meat, dumplings boiled in a sheet,
   Dandelion and crackies' teeth at the Kelligrews _____.

8. Come and sit by my side if you love me,
   Do not hasten to bid me adieu,
   But remember the _____ _____ _____
   And the girl who has loved you so true.

FOOD & DRINK

38. Atlantic Dishes

Here are some of the dishes to order or prepare when in Atlantic Canada. Notes on the cuisine are based on those supplied by William B. Hamilton of Halifax. The names of the dishes appear on the left, their ingredients and countries of origin on the right. Match them up to find out what you should be relishing!

1. Bannock.

    A. Chicken and leek soup (Scottish).

2. Brewis.

    B. Potatoes and salt cod fish covered with a dressing of salt pork scraps and onions (German).

3. Cock-a-leekie.

    C. Potato patties filled with pieces of lean pork (Acadian).

4. Dutch Mess.

    D. A blend of cabbage, turnips, and potatoes; Colcannon (Irish).

5. Fanikaneekins.

    E. An oatmeal cake (Scottish).

6. Finnan Haddie.

    F. Steamed fruit pudding (United Empire Loyalist, American).

7. Kohl Cannon.

    G. Bite-sized chunks of haddock cured with smoke of green wood (Scottish).

8. Pâté à la Râpure.

    H. Grated potatoes layered with chicken or beef (Acadian).

9. Poutines Râpées.

    I. Boiled ship's biscuit with codfish (sometimes with potatoes and wild herbs) (English via Newfoundland).

10. Sailors Duff.

    J. Yeast buns sprinkled with sugar (English).

11. Sally Lunn.

    K. Salt herring marinated in vinegar, pickling sauce, and onions; salamagundi (German).

12. Solomon Grundy.

    L. Pieces of freshly risen bread dough fried in hot fat and served with maple syrup or molasses (German).

39. Drink Up!

There are a number of distinctive drinks associated with Canada. The purpose of this quiz is to whet — not quench — your thirst for our national beverages!

1. Newfoundlanders have a taste for Screech. What is it?
2. Winnipeg goldeye is not the same as Calgary red-eye. How are they different?
3. Two West Coast institutions are Rogers Chocolates and Murchie's Tea and Coffee Ltd. Rogers' large pure-cream chocolates come in bright red _____ and are shipped all over the world. Murchie's blend their own teas, and one of the most popular is Empress _____ Tea, named after the famed hotel in _____, B.C.
4. Calona Wines is the largest winery in British Columbia. It was started in 1931 and its first president was _____, who went on to become premier of the province.
5. Canada's largest winery is Bright's Wines which makes use of the vines of the _____ area.
6. What is the name of the world's best-selling wine, both nationally and internationally? It is a sparkling red, medium dry wine, with seven per cent alcohol content. It is made by Andrès.
7. The cow that set the world record for butterfat production, Springbank Snow Countess, produced 4,112 kg (9,062 lbs) of butterfat, a world record, between 1919 and 1936. To commemorate the feat, a statue of the cow was erected in her hometown, _____, Ont.
8. In the North, moosemilk is slang for one of two beverages. Name one or both.
9. What does the "V.O." stand for on the label of Seagram's V.O.? And, while asking such questions, what does the Latin motto *Ne Plus Ultra* mean?
10. Seagram's V.O. is the largest selling brand of whisky in the United States, and the world's largest-selling Canadian whisky. It is a _____ whisky derived from rye grain from the Province of _____.
11. Hiram Walker-Gooderham and Worts Ltd., of _____, Ont., distill "the world's lightest whisky." This is popular around the world, and a reason for its continued popularity has been the advertising campaign that since 1946 has identified the drink with adventurers in out-of-the-way places. The name of the whisky is _____.
12. Two non-alcoholic, orange-flavored drinks have a Toronto connection. One is Orange _____, which is bottled world-wide, but owned and managed from Toronto. Another is _____, which is a local product, a syrupy drink dispensed at Murray's Restaurants and the Canadian National Exhibition.
13. A world-famous soft drink was developed in Toronto by John J. McLaughlin, brother of Sam McLaughlin of McLaughlin-Buick fame. What is it called?
14. Over 115 brands of beer are brewed in Canada by some forty-four breweries. The best selling beer in Canada is Labatt's _____.
15. In addition to the national brands brewed by major companies like Carling O'Keefe, Labatt's, and Molson's, there are regional brands brewed by local operations (and often owned by the major companies). Here are some local

brands. If you are drinking them, in which province or region would you likely be?

A. India Pale Ale Malt Liquor.
B. Schooner Beer and Old Scotia Ale.
C. Lethbridge Royal Stout.
D. Moosehead Premium Ale.
E. Kakabeka Cream Lager and Silver Spray Beer.
F. Kokanee Pilsener Beer.
G. White Seal Beer.

16. The quintessential Canadian toast, which is of Indian-Inuit derivation, is: "_____!"

---

40. Eat Up!

This set of questions is based on the food we eat. We should be more conscious of what it is we consume. Maybe this quiz will help us to focus attention on our foodstuff.

1. Camembec, Oka, and Anfrom are three varieties of _____ that come from the Province of _____.

2. If Beefalo is a tasty cross between buffalo and cattle (or as someone once put it "a cross between Elsie the Cow and Ferdinand the Bull"), what is Yakallo?

3. Reindeer herds were shepherded by Eskimos in the 1920s for the production of reindeer meat. True or false.

4. What variety of hard, smooth, nippy cheese, first commercially produced in Ingersoll, Ont., at the time of Confederation, is popular in Canada and eaten around the world? What is a milder variety called?

5. Children a few generations ago ate and also collected what the O-Pee-Chee Co. Ltd. of London, Ont. produced. What was the product?

6. Since the 1930s, the leading brand of Canadian cigarette has been manufactured by Macdonald Tobacco Inc. of Montreal. What is the name of the popular brand?

7. A red apple that is juicy, crisp, and sweet was first grown on a small farm in Dundas County in present-day Ontario in 1811. It was named after the farmer, John _____, who domesticated the original tree. What is the name of that apple?

8. Uneasy with the connotations of the word, Saskatchewan farmers gave a new name to rapeseed. What did they call it?

9. James H. _____ established a family business in 1872 in a small bakery and candy shop in St. Stephen, N.B. The business expanded rapidly and by 1910 was selling the five-cent chocolate bar which it pioneered. Today it is Canada's only privately owned, large confectionery company. What is the last name of the founder, and what is the name of the company he founded?

10. In the 1940s and 1950s, when a French Canadian asked for "Un Mae West et un Pepsi," he wanted:

A. A girlie magazine and a Coke.
B. A hot dog and a soft-drink.
C. A sugar-roll and a Pepsi-Cola.
D. A frankfurter and a Pepsi-Cola.

11. Fiddleheads are a delicacy grown in what province in particular?

12. The world's tastiest edible seaweed, called _____, comes from Lake Dark Harbour on New Brunswick's Grand Manan Island. Fill in the blank.

13. The world's largest single wheatfield — some 35,000 acres — was first sown in 1951. It is located near _____, Alta.

14. Wes McKnight used to extol the merits of "that grand tasting energy food" which he identified as Bee Hive Golden _____. Complete the brand name.

15. *Riz du Canada* on a Paris menu identifies:
    A. Brown rice from Lac du Riz, Valleyfield, Que.
    B. White rice from Rice Lake, Annapolis Valley, N.S.
    C. Wild rice from Rice Lake, Peterborough, Ont.

16. Eskimo Ice Cream is a delicacy supposedly prepared by the Eskimos, consisting of cooked meat, melted tallow, blueberries, and whitefish kneaded in snow until frozen. True or false.

17. Pemmican is preserved buffalo or caribou meat and was a food staple of the fur trade and the Plains Indians. True or false.

18. Thousand Islands Dressing is named after the islands in the St. Lawrence River. True or false.

19. Dr. Archibald Huntsman of the Biological Board of Canada should be remembered when one recalls the name of Clarence Birdseye. Why?

20. Dr. Frederick Tisdall developed _____ Biscuits, with irradiated Vitamin D, manufactured by Manning Biscuit Corporation. Fill in the trade name.

21. What is jerky, which is commonly eaten in the Yukon.

22. As the saying goes, "If the Americans had won the War of 1812, we would be eating Fanny Farmer chocolates now." What do we eat instead?

FRENCH FACT

41. Going Places

In French, Ontario is spelled Ontario, Alberta remains Alberta, but British Columbia is _____. Give the French forms for the following provinces and territories.

1. British Columbia.
2. New Brunswick.
3. Newfoundland.
4. Northwest Territories.
5. Nova Scotia.
6. Prince Edward Island.
7. Province of Quebec.
8. Yukon Territory.

42. How Fluent Is Your French?

Below you will find thirty common English words and phrases. What are their French equivalents?

1. Please.
2. Thank you.
3. Why?
4. How are you?
5. Who is it?
6. Good-bye.
7. Good evening.
8. What time is it?
9. Maybe.
10. Of course.
11. Really!
12. Listen well.
13. Congratulations!
14. At last!
15. Bravo!
16. I love you.
17. Here's the bathroom.
18. No smoking.
19. Ladies and gentlemen.
20. Hurry up!
21. Wake up.
22. Good luck!
23. It's a secret.
24. Once upon a time. . .
25. It's difficult.
26. Don't cry.
27. I understand.
28. Calm down.
29. Go away.
30. I am bilingual.

43. Bilingual Buying

One of the characteristics of a Canadian at breakfast is that, besides eating bacon and eggs, he takes the time to read the print on the cereal box, twice — once in English, once again in French. Sometimes the words mean the same thing, sometimes not. One of the pleasures of supermarket shopping is trying to identify the no-name packaged goods by their labels in French. Here are some products. What are they?

1. Biscuits fondants beurre d'arachides.
2. Confiture de framboises.
3. Détergent de lave-vaisselle automatique.
4. Dîner macaroni au fromage.
5. Essuie tout.
6. Fèves au lard.
7. Gruau rapide.
8. Jus de tomate.
9. Marbrée au caramel écossais crème glacée.
10. Mélange pour pâté à crêpes.
11. Mouchoirs de papier.
12. Nettoyeur à vitres.
13. Papier hygiénique.
14. Poivre noir, moulu.
15. Poudre d'aïl.
16. Purée des pommes.
17. Riz soufflé.
18. Sirop de maïs doré.
19. Vinaigre blanc.
20. Vinaigrette Mille-Iles.

44. How Fluent is Your English?

From your answers to the questions asked earlier in this section, it is apparent how much French you know. From the questions that follow, it will become apparent how fluent you are in English — and in translating everyday driving terms from one official language into another. What do these terms mean in English?

1. Cul-de-sac.
2. Défense de doubler.
3. Au secours!
4. Panne d'essence.
5. Déviation.
6. Pont en réparation.
7. Sens interdit.
8. Sens unique.
9. Cédez.
10. Arrêt.

45. General Questions

These are general-knowledge questions in the field of Canadiana. Some are difficult, others easy.

1. Since Confederation there have been three prime ministers from French Canada. Name them.
2. Ewan McColl and Peggy Seeger composed a ballad about an incident that occurred in the Maritimes in 1958. What was the incident?
3. Who boasted: "I am the first prime minister of this country of neither altogether English nor French origin"?
4. Name the birthplace of Snorri, son of Thorfinnr and Guidridr.
5. What new land did the Dominion of Canada acquire in 1869?
6. "Skunk" is the Algonkian word for "a smelly weasel." What is the skunk called in the southern United States?
7. Who was the American general who died during the attack on Quebec in 1775?
8. In the Canadian West, what was referred to as a "sky pilot"?
9. Which agreement limits naval armaments on the Great Lakes?
10. To a Maritimer, what is a "tickle"?
11. Who was the French cynic who maintained that the English and the French were at war over "a few acres of snow"?
12. Where is there "no place for the state," according to Pierre Elliott Trudeau, then minister of justice?
13. To the English it was Fort Ticonderoga, to the French Fort-Carillon. On which lake was this fort located?
14. The LSR was an influential group of socialists active in the 1930s. What do the initials represent?
15. In the United States it is the Surgeon General who advises that cigarette smoking may be hazardous to health. In Canada who "advises that danger to health increases with amount smoked. Avoid inhaling"?

16. Canada Post replies to letters addressed to Santa Claus, North Pole, Canada, with the appropriate postal code. What is the appropriate postal code for Santa Claus?

17. What is a baby beaver called?

18. Members of which profession are encouraged to wear an iron ring?

19. What is the name of the cartoon character known as "the imp of the ice lanes" created by Hanna-Barbera?

20. "Connie" is the nickname of which airplane flown in the 1950s by Air Canada?

21. How does the Peter Principle go?

22. One of the specialized agencies of the United Nations is located in Montreal, but which one?

23. What are the names of the so-called Three Wise Men of Canadian politics?

24. What is a *ceinture fléchée*?

25. What is MURB?

26. What is the name of the world's longest paved highway which extends from Victoria to St. John's?

27. Did Milt Schmidt play hockey with the Detroit Red Wings or the Boston Bruins?

28. Which Canadian city today has the largest concentration of Chinese?

29. Which Maritime government assisted in the production of the ill-fated Bricklin?

30. What is the name of the Indian nation formed by these five groups: Kutchin, Hare, Slavey, Dogrib, Chipewyan?

31. What was learned about the English-Wabigoon River system in Ontario in the Spring of 1970?

32. What popular game do some sports historians believe was first played in Kingston on Christmas Day, 1855?

33. How many seats are there in the House of Commons?

34. Which group devised 5BX and 10BX?

35. What is the basic difference between 5BX and 10BX?

36. In what peninsula is located the Chubb crater?

37. What is the last name of Sam the Record Man?

38. Which is longer, a quarter mile or a quarter kilometre?

39. Who was named first Governor of New France on 23 May 1633?

40. What do the Inuit call the cairn constructed of rock that resembles the outline of a human figure?

41. Which is the most northern of the provinces?

42. He died at the Royal Columbian Hospital on 28 June 1981, but in a sense this heroic young man did not die, for his Marathon of Hope continues. Name him.

43. Which act of government guarantees Canadians "Laws for the Peace, Order, and Good Government of Canada"?

44. What national magazine has had as its editor Thomas B. Costain, Ralph Allen, Blair Fraser, Ken Lefolii, Charles Templeton, Peter Gzowski, and Peter C. Newman?

45. In Nova Scotia, a fungy is: a fish stew, a soggy moss, or a blueberry pie?

46. Name the Canadian general who was appointed in 1917 to command the Canadian Corps.

47. Which British-born, Canadian humorist once said, about an imaginary character, that "he rode madly off in all directions"?

48. Josiah Henson, who settled in Upper Canada in 1830, was the model of which famous literary character?

49. Toronto was once an outpost of the French empire. What then was its name?

50. On the armorial bearings of Canada, does the unicorn stand to the left of the shield or to the right?

51. The name of which Western province means, in Cree, "Strait of the Spirit"?

52. What occurred that caused much comment and inconvenience in northeastern Canada and the United States on 9 and 10 November 1965?

53. The North American moose is almost the same as what European animal?

54. In 1949, in the Province of Quebec, a bitter strike broke out. In which town did it take place?

55. Name the two Canadian dancers who placed first in duet ensemble at the International Ballet Competition in Moscow in 1973.

56. Who directed the feature film *Goin' Down the Road*?

57. The Strait of Canso separates which land masses?

58. The Senate has how many members?

59. Who is the Whitehorse-born author and media personality who once said, "A Canadian is somebody who knows how to make love in a canoe"?

60. In which city will you find the plaque with the following inscription: "Providence being their guide / They builded better than they knew"?

---

46. The Toughest Questions

This set is composed of questions that are, at least in the opinion of the question-setter, the most difficult in the book. Some of the questions turn on a knowledge of trivia, yet some people believe that one man's trivia is another man's treasure. Still, it could scarcely be said that these questions are in the realm of general knowledge. Anyway, there are a baker's dozen here, and the average person is expected to answer one. Thus forewarned, see how well you fare!

1. Canada came into existence on 1 July 1867. What day of the week was that?

2. FANY is a Second World War acronym. It means First Aid Nursing Yeomanry, but it was a cover for what operation?

3. A Canadian woman was the first person to appear on the *world's* first television program. What was her name?

4. Before becoming a famous novelist, Brian Moore wrote two Harlequin Romances under pseudonyms. What are the two pseudonyms?

5. What were W.L. Mackenzie King's dying words?

6. Identify and name the "Symphony Six."

7. Betsy Ross sewed the first American flag. What is the name of the Ottawa woman who did the same for the new Maple Leaf flag?

8. Chinook Jargon was spoken on the West Coast. What was the *lingua franca* of the Red River area in Manitoba in the 19th century?

9. What was Naomi Uemura's accomplishment of heroic proportions in 1978?

10. Name the Canadian-born sculptor of the brace of stately lions that guard the New York Public Library.

11. Alexander Graham Bell had a more melodious way of greeting callers on the telephone than the traditional "Hello," which he found unappealing. What did he say?

12. What is the name of the Canadian-born announcer who introduces from New York the Metropolitan Opera Broadcasts on CBC Radio?

13. Where is Canada Bay?

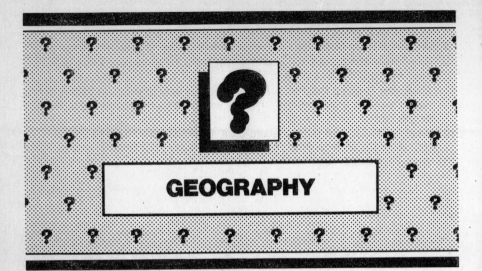

GEOGRAPHY

47. Geography in General

1. Canada occupies which of the two hemispheres?
2. On which of the seven continents of the world is Canada located?
3. Which province is the largest? Which is the smallest?
4. Canada has one of the lowest population densities of all the countries in the world — 6 persons per 259 ha (square mile). (Excluding the Yukon Territory and the Northwest Territories, the figure is 10 persons per 259 ha.) Which province has the highest density?
5. Name the three districts that make up the Northwest Territories.
6. Name three provinces untouched by any American states.
7. What are the geographical or physiographical characteristics of the following points?
   A. Middle Island, Lake Erie.
   B. Cape Columbia, Ellesmere Island, N.W.T.
   C. Cape Spear, Nfld.
   D. Mount St. Elias, Y.T.
8. Eskimo Point, on the west coast of Hudson Bay, is the geographical _____ of Canada — that is, the point of balance of a map of Canada cut from a large globe.
9. Nine out of ten Canadians live within 320 kilometres (200 miles) of the U.S.-Canadian border. True or false.
10. The United States is Canada's closest neighbor, for the two countries share some boundary lines. The largest but least populous of the American states touches Canada. This is the state of _____, the capital of which is _____. With what part of Canada does it share a border?
11. In the Gulf of St. Lawrence, some 24 km (15 miles) off the southern tip of Newfoundland, lie two islands. What are their names and of what country are they possessions? The approximate area of the two islands is a) 1931 ha (9 square miles); b) 20,087 ha (93 square miles); c) 45,987 ha (193 square miles). And what is Langlade?

12. From a hill near Alert, on the northeastern tip of Ellesmere Island, the most eastern of the Arctic Islands, it is possible to see in the distance the mountains of a foreign land. This is the island of _____, a province of which kingdom?

13. Another of Canada's neighbors has as its northernmost region _____, a name that comes from *Sibir,* which means "sleeping land." Name the country.

48. Water Everywhere

Water. *L'eau.* Aqua pura. H_2O. Adam's ale. The elixir of life. Call it what you wish — water is essential to existence. Luckily, Canada is well-endowed with water. To find out how well, answer these questions about the precious fluid.

1. Canada has more freshwater than any other country in the world, with the exception of the Soviet Union. True or false.

2. The St. Lawrence River is the longest river in Canada. True or false.

3. The Great Lakes is the largest group of lakes in the world. True or false.

4. By estimate, Canada has the following percentage of the freshwater in the world:
   A. One-eighth.
   B. One-seventh.
   C. One-sixth.
   D. One-fifth.
   E. One-fourth.

5. Which province or territory has the greatest area of freshwater?

6. British Columbia has approximately ten times the freshwater area Ontario has. True or false.

7. The highest waterfall in Canada is Takkakaw Falls, which has a drop of 380 metres (1,248 feet). Takkakaw Falls is located in which province or territory?

8. The largest lake in Canada is _____.

9. Three rivers run through the city of Ottawa. The Ottawa River and the Gatineau River are two. Name the third.

10. Which two bodies of water are connected by:
    A. The Soo Lock?
    B. The Welland Canal?

11. What is the name of the bay that is part of Lake Huron?

12. What makes Saskatchewan's Lake Manitou notable and unique among the country's water bodies?

13. The highest tides in the world are recorded in the Bay of _____, which separates New _____ and Nova _____.

14. Niagara Falls has been called the most famous cataract in the world. It is composed of two separate cascades. What are the names of these falls?

15. The British poet Rupert Brooke, traveling across Canada in 1913, characterized the Great Lakes thus: "They are too big, and too smooth, and too sunny; like an American _____." Complete the sentence.

49. What Province is This?

Below appear outlines of each of the provinces and territories in Canada. Identify them.

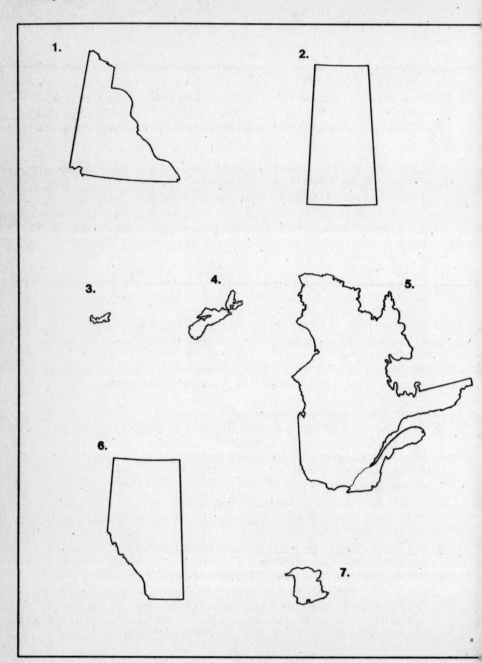

1.

2.

3.

4.

5.

6.

7.

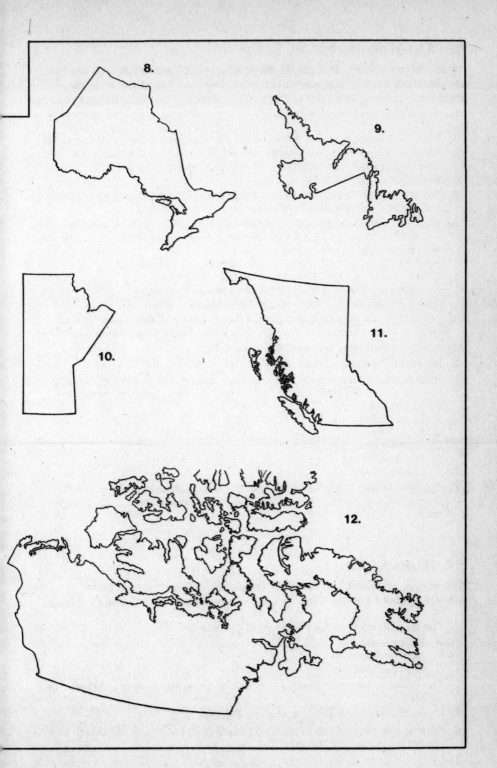

8.

9.

10.

11.

12.

50. On Mountains

"A sea of mountains" is a phrase associated with Canada's fourth sea (after the Atlantic, Pacific, and Arctic Oceans). The "sea" in question is the Rocky Mountains. You may be "at sea" with the following questions, which are all about Canada's mountains.

1. The first European to see the Rocky Mountains was Anthony Henday. The event occurred near present-day Innisfail, Alta., on 17 October 1754. The following phrase is associated with that experience: "Behold! The _____ Mountains." Fill in the blank.

2. The ten highest mountains in Canada are all located within the borders of British Columbia and the Yukon Territory. True or false.

3. We know Canada's highest mountain is Mount Logan in the Yukon, and that it is 6050 metres (19,850 feet) high. How does Mount Logan compare with Mount Everest? Mount Logan is:
   A. 2,798 metres (9,178 feet) higher than Mount Everest.
   B. 2,798 metres (9,178 feet) shorter than Mount Everest.
   C. 54.25 metres (178 feet) higher than Mount Everest.
   D. 54.25 metres (178 feet) shorter than Mount Everest.

4. In which range may be found the following: Mount Clemenceau, The Helmet, Bush Mountain, Mount St. Alexander, and Odaray Mountain?

5. In which range may be found Blow-me-Down?

6. Mount Tremblant is part of which range?

7. Here are six mountains — four are imaginary or non-existent in Canada; two are actual Canadian peaks. Which are the real Canadian mountains?
   A. Mount Bumpus.
   B. Mount Edison.
   C. Eiffel Peak.
   D. Fleming Mountain.
   E. Moriyama Peak.
   F. Mount Sorrel.

8. The best-known Canadian book with the word "mountain" in its title is Ernest Buckler's 1952 novel titled *The Mountain and the* _____. Fill in the blank.

---

51. Islands Ahoy

"No man is an island," wrote John Donne, but all men should know something about islands. Here is a set of questions about Canada's islands.

1. The largest island in the Dominion of Canada is:
   A. Baffin Island.
   B. Newfoundland.
   C. Vancouver Island.

2. The island of Newfoundland is about three times the area of Labrador. True or false.

3. Name the largest island on Canada's Pacific Coast.

4. What is the name of the large island that lies in the mouth of Hudson Bay? (Its name begins with the letter S.)

5. Which is the largest of the Arctic Islands?

6. Manitoulin Island, in Georgian Bay, is the largest _____ island in the world.

7. Both Newfoundland on the East Coast and Vancouver Island on the West Coast are islands. Which is the larger of the two?

8. Which is bigger: Baffin Island or Newfoundland including Labrador?

9. The ten largest islands in Canada are all in the Northwest Territories and Newfoundland? True or false.

10. Name the first island to be colonized.

11. The motto of a newspaper in the Maritimes is "Covers the Island like the Dew." Which island is the reference to?

12. "The Great Island" is the unofficial motto of _____.

GOVERNMENT

52. The Monarchy

Canada is both a dominion and a monarchy. Unlike the United States, which is a Republic with a president at its head, Canada is a kingdom with a sovereign. For centuries the French and British sovereigns fought to rule over this country. Canada has been a colony of France and of England. It is now an independent country with the sovereign of the United Kingdom as its supreme authority. Here is a set of questions based on the monarchs of Canada.

1. This list of the kings and queens of Great Britain and Canada since 1867 appears in alphabetical order. Rearrange the list to make it correspond to the order of their reigns.

   A. Edward VII.   i. 1837-1901.
   B. Edward VIII.   ii. 1901-10.
   C. Elizabeth II.   iii. 1910-36.
   D. George V.   iv. 1936.
   E. George VI.   v. 1936-1952.
   F. Queen Victoria. vi. 1952 to present.

2. He was the son of Louis the Fourteenth, the Sun King. He was the last of the French monarchs of Early Canada. "Are the streets being paved with gold over there?" he complained when presented with the costs incurred in building the Fortress of Louisbourg. "I fully expect to wake one morning in Versailles to see the walls of the fortress rising above the horizon." Nevertheless, the Fortress was named after him. What was his name?

3. Was George I, George II, or George III on the British throne when Quebec fell to General Wolfe in 1759?

4. Edward VIII, as the Prince of _____, toured Canada in 1919 and broke royal precedent by acquiring land in one of the dominions. The ranch he bought was located in the Province of _____. Following his abdication in 1936, he acquired the title, Duke of _____.

5. The first Royal Visit of a reigning monarch was made by King _____ VI, and Queen _____, who crossed the country in their royal blue train May and June of 1939, a few months before the outbreak of _____.

6. The official designation of the sovereign is: "Elizabeth the Second, by the _____, of the United Kingdom, Canada and Her other Realms and Territories, Queen, Head of _____, Defender of the _____."

7. Queen Elizabeth II is married to Philip _____, Duke of _____. The Queen and her _____ have four children. The children of the Royal Family are named: Prince Charles, Princess _____, Prince Andrew, and Prince _____.

8. Prince Charles is the heir apparent. His title is the Prince of _____. When he toured the Eastern Arctic in 1974, the Eskimos of that region called him *Attaniout Ikeneego*, which translates: "The Son of the Big _____."

9. According to the BNA Act of 1867, the "authority of and over Canada" is vested in _____, the representative of which in a self-governing dominion is called _____.

10. "The principle that the monarch is able to do virtually nothing without the authorization of his or her constitutional advisers, the cabinet, who are responsible to Parliament, is known as. . . ."
    A. The Monarchical Principle.
    B. The Constitutional Monarchy.
    C. Absolutism.

11. When you are introduced to the Queen, refer to her, initially, as _____, and then, later, as _____.

53. Who Was the P.M. Then?

Americans are inclined to think of world events as occurring during presidential administrations; Britons, during reigns of sovereigns. Do Canadians view world events from the vantagepoint of their prime ministers? If it is easy to answer these questions, then we do; if answering them is like pulling hen's teeth, then we do not.

1. Who was prime minister on 22 November 1963, the day President Kennedy was assassinated?

2. Who was prime minister in October and November of 1929 when the stock market crashed and the Great Depression began?

3. Who was prime minister when the first atomic bomb was dropped, on Hiroshima, 6 August 1945?

4. Who was prime minister on 17 December 1903, the day the Wright Brothers flew the first heavier-than-air craft at Kitty Hawk?

5. Who was prime minister at the death of Marshall Stalin in the Kremlin, Moscow, 6 March 1953?

6. Who was prime minister when the Russian Revolution broke out, 7 November 1917?

7. Who was prime minister when General Wolseley's expedition arrived in Khartoum in a vain attempt to save General Gordon, January 1885?

8. Who was prime minister on 22 January 1901, the day that Queen Victoria died?

9. Who was governor general — not prime minister, this time — when Neil Armstrong went for his "moon walk," 20 July 1969?

54. Prime Ministers

In a self-governing dominion, the prime minister is the head of the government. Below appear the terms of office of the prime ministers of Canada, with about half the names filled in. From general knowledge, fill in the rest.

1. 1867-1873.
2. 1873-1878.
3. 1878-1891. Sir John A. Macdonald.
4. 1891-1892. Sir John Abbott.
5. 1892-1894. Sir John Thompson.
6. 1894-1896. Sir Mackenzie Bowell.
7. 1896.
8. 1896-1911.
9. 1911-1920. Sir Robert Borden.
10. 1920-1921. Arthur Meighen.
11. 1921-1926. W.L. Mackenzie King.
12. 1926.
13. 1926-1930. W.L. Mackenzie King.
14. 1930-1935.
15. 1935-1948.
16. 1948-1957. Louis St. Laurent.
17. 1957-1963.
18. 1963-1968. Lester B. Pearson.
19. 1968-1979. Pierre Elliott Trudeau.
20. 1979-80.
21. 1980-

55. Who's Who: Prime Ministers

The prime minister is the head of the federal government in a self-governing dominion and in practice the leader of the party in power in the lower house of the legislature. Since Confederation, sixteen men (and no women) have served in this capacity. How recognizable are these gentlemen from their photographs? Match their photos (which appear in no special order) with their names (given here in the order in which they served, along with party allegiance — C for Conservative, L for Liberal).

A. Sir John A. Macdonald (C).
B. Alexander Mackenzie (L).
C. Sir John Abbott (C).
D. Sir John Thompson (C).
E. Sir Mackenzie Bowell (C).
F. Sir Charles Tupper (C).
G. Sir Wilfrid Laurier (L).
H. Sir Robert Borden (C).
I. Arthur Meighen (C).
J. W.L. Mackenzie King (L).
K. R.B. Bennett (C).
L. Louis St. Laurent (L).
M. John G. Diefenbaker (C).
N. Lester B. Pearson (L).
O. Pierre Elliott Trudeau (L).
P. Joe Clark (C).

1. **2.** **3.** **4.**

5. **6.** **7.** **8.**

9. **10.** **11.** **12.**

13. **14.** **15.** **16.**

55

56. Who's Who: Governors General

The representative of the crown in Canada and the head of state is called the governor general. The office is symbolic of national unity and the continuity of institutions and national life. It dates back to 1786 and, in its modern form, from 1867. The incumbent was invariably a titled Britisher until 1952. Here are photographs of eleven men (no women as yet!) who have held the highest appointed office in the land. From the clue matching the photo number, identify the incumbent. (Should the clues seem somewhat frivolous, recall that one "G.G." — Vincent Massey — referred to his duties as consisting largely of "governor generalities.")

1. Rhymes with a kind of Aspirin. Lord _____.
2. Donated a famous cup.
3. Donated a national challenge cup.
4. This Lord rhymes with King (with whom he feuded).
5. Suggests: Good Queen . . . Rotten . . . Lord _____.
6. Wrote thrillers.
7. Not Raymond Harris-Ferguson. "He made the Crown Canadian."
8. Distinguished war hero. Major-General RAVINE (unscramble).
9. Name recalls that of Lord Kitchener.
10. Means "light" or "frivolous" in French.
11. Edward CEEHRRSY.

1.　　　　2.

3.

4.

5.

6.

7.

8.

9.

10.

11.

57. Royal Commissions

Appointed by federal or provincial governments to make impartial inquiries into pressing problems, royal commissions are often identified with the names of the commissioners appointed to head them, rather than by their descriptive titles. Can you remember — or imagine — what each commissioner or commissioners would inquire about?

1. Mrs. Florence Bird studied:
   A. The position and prospects of Canadian magazines.
   B. The status of women.
   C. Health services.
2. Thomas Berger analyzed:
   A. Espionage in Canada.
   B. Canada's economic prospects.
   C. The Mackenzie Valley pipeline.
3. Kenneth Carter looked at:
   A. Taxation in Canada.
   B. Dominion-provincial relations.
   C. Price spreads in Canada.
4. Walter L. Gordon concerned himself with:
   A. Canada's economic prospects.
   B. National development in the arts, letters, and sciences.
   C. The position and prospects of Canadian magazines.
5. Emmett Hall looked into:
   A. The status of women.
   B. Health services.
   C. Bilingualism and biculturalism.
6. André Laurendeau and Davidson Dunton were enamored of:
   A. The position and prospects of Canadian magazines.
   B. The Mackenzie Valley pipeline.
   C. Bilingualism and biculturalism.
7. Vincent Massey was bothered about:
   A. Espionage in Canada.
   B. National development in the arts, letters and sciences.
   C. Price spreads in Canada.
8. Grattan O'Leary was exercised over:
   A. The position and prospects of Canadian magazines.
   B. Canada's economic prospects.
   C. Taxation in Canada.
9. Newton Rowell and Joseph Sirois inquired into:
   A. The status of women.
   B. Bilingualism and biculturalism.
   C. Dominion-provincial relations.
10. R.L. Kellock and Robert Taschereau took notes on:
   A. Espionage in Canada.

B. Health services.

C. The Mackenzie Valley pipeline.

11. H.H. Stevens tabled his report on:

A. National development in the arts, letters and sciences.

B. Taxation in Canada.

C. Price spreads in Canada.

HISTORY

58. Fields of Honor

Canadians are a peace-loving people, yet many Canadians have had to fight on fields of honor. Here are a few sites of important battles. Answer the questions below by spotting the right answers or eliminating the incorrect ones.

1. Who fought in the Battle of Châteauguay in 1813?
   - A. The British regulars and the Canadian militia.
   - B. The French-Canadian *voltigeurs* and the militia.
   - C. Brigadier-General Richard Montgomery.

2. Who won the Battle of Lundy's Lane, the scene of the bloodiest fighting in the War of 1812?
   - A. British and Canadian soldiers.
   - B. American soldiers.
   - C. Neither British and Canadian nor American soldiers.

3. In present-day terms, where was the Battle of Batoche of 1885 fought?
   - A. At Batoche, on the South Saskatchewan River, Sask.
   - B. At Batoche, twenty kilometres north of Regina, Sask.
   - C. At present-day Prince Albert, Sask.

4. What happened at the Second Battle of Ypres, 1915?
   - A. The First Canadian Contingent succumbed to the first gas attack in modern history.
   - B. The First Canadian Contingent survived the first gas attack in modern history.
   - C. The German Army attacked the Canadian salient and broke through.

5. Who commanded the Canadian Corps at Vimy Ridge, 1917?
   - A. Lt.-Gen. Julian Byng.
   - B. Lt.-Gen. Sir Arthur Currie.
   - C. Col. William Otter.

6. What was the ultimate value of the Dieppe Raid, 1942?
   A. The Second Canadian Division established its beachhead.
   B. The raid proved the fighting worth of Canadian troops.
   C. Experience was gained in the planning of the Normandy invasion.

59. Momentous Dates

Each date that follows marks the occurrence of a momentous event in Canada's history. What historical event took place on each day?

1.	2 May 1670.	**6.**	14 April 1917.
2.	13 September 1759.	**7.**	11 November 1918.
3.	1 July 1867.	**8.**	15 May 1919.
4.	16 November 1885.	**9.**	10 September 1939.
5.	17 August 1896.	**10.**	5 October 1970.

60. Historic Quotations

Historic events usually inspire memorable quotations. Here are some important quotations connected with events in the Canadian past and present. Recall the name of the speaker and identify the event that inspired him or her to utter the words in question.

1. "Gentlemen," exclaimed _____, "I would rather have written those lines than take Quebec tomorrow."
2. "Alexander _____, from Canada, by land, the twenty-second of July, one thousand seven hundred and ninety-three," he painted on the rock.
3. "Push on, brave York Volunteers!" was _____'s dying command.
4. "I expected to find a contest between a government and a people," wrote _____. "I found two nations warring in the bosom of a single state."
5. "Stand fast, Craigellachie!" telegraphed _____.
6. "I say humbly, through the grace of God I believe I am the prophet of the New World," admitted _____.
7. "Not necessarily conscription but conscription if necessary," mumbled _____.
8. "The grim fact is that we prepare for war like precocious giants and for peace like retarded pygmies," orated _____.
9. "Vive le Québec! Vive le Québec libre!" declaimed _____.
10. "When I scored that final goal," bragged _____, "I finally realized what democracy was all about."
11. "I have never been so proud as tonight to be a Québècois," murmured _____.
12. "It wasn't my intention to become a hero," exclaimed _____. "I just did what anyone would do in the same situation."

61. Explorers and Discoverers

The history of early Canada is the story of the country being opened up by courageous and determined explorers and discoverers. The names of these men have gone down in history, though their achievements are appreciated largely by historians. This set of questions turns on the expeditions of these explorers and discoverers by focusing on what they are principally remembered for. Match up the explorer with his main accomplishment.

Part One

1. John Cabot, an Italian mariner in the service of England, four years after Columbus's famous voyage . . .

2. Jacques Cartier, the navigator from the French seaport of Saint-Malo, in 1534 . . .

3. Sir Martin Frobisher, the English mariner, made his first . . .

4. Samuel de Champlain, the French explorer and "Father of New France" . . .

5. Henry Hudson, the English navigator, aboard the *Discovery*, in 1610 . . .

6. Pierre-Esprit Radisson, along with his brother-in-law Sieur des Groseilliers, *coureurs de bois* . . .

A. lived at Port Royal in 1605, in Quebec in 1608, and explored Lake Champlain, Georgian Bay, and Lake Huron.

B. explored Lake Superior in 1659 and were among the founders of the Hudson's Bay Company.

C. explored Hudson Bay and James Bay, searching for a route to Cathay.

D. Arctic voyage in 1576. He gave Baffin Island its present name and explored Frobisher Bay (which he thought was a strait).

E. explored the Gulf of St. Lawrence and voyaged as far as present-day Quebec City and Montreal.

F. examined the North American coast from Maine to Newfoundland's Cape Race.

Part Two

7. Comte de Frontenac, Governor of New France from 1672 to 1678 . . .

8. Cavelier de La Salle, French-born seigneur, built . . .

9. Samuel Hearne, explorer in the employ of the fur trade, 1771-72 . . .

10. Captain James Cook, master of the Royal Navy, in 1778 . . .

11. Sir Alexander Mackenzie, fur trader and explorer, in 1789 set out to . . .

A. explored the West Coast through the Bering Strait to Icy Cape (70°N) on Chukchi Sea (Arctic Ocean).

B. down the Fraser River to its tidewater, mistakenly believing it to be the Columbia River.

C. and charted the Columbia River to its mouth, and ultimately mapped two million square miles of North America.

D. fostered French expansion throughout North America and the construction of fur-trade posts in the West.

E. Fort Frontenac at Cataraqui (later Kingston) and in 1682 sailed down the Mississippi and discovered Louisiana.

12. Simon Fraser, another fur trader and explorer, in 1808, voyaged . . .

13. David Thompson, explorer and geographer, in 1811, descended . . .

F. explore the river that now bears his name. He went on to cross Canada by land four years later.

G. found the Coppermine River and became the first white man to reach the Arctic Ocean overland.

---

62. Disastrous Dates

Disasters, whether natural or man-made, are timeless in the sense that they may occur any time and any place. They are always unexpected. The dates that follow are those on which specific disasters occurred. With each date there is a clue to what happened. What happened on each date?

1. 5 February 1663. It took place on land.
2. 29 April 1903. It involved land.
3. 29 May 1914. It took place on water.
4. 3 February 1916. It concerned one of the elements.
5. 6 December 1917. It took place in a port city.
6. 19 May 1950. It concerned one of the elements.
7. 15 October 1954. It concerned the atmosphere.
8. 23 October 1958. It took place underground.

---

63. Least-Liked Men

The RCMP distributes a "most-wanted" list of criminals. Here is a "least-liked" list of men and women, some of whom were criminals, some of whom were not. All of them were hated, reviled, and detested in their day. Some are still despised; others have been forgiven. Some divided the population; others united it against themselves. Some are infamous for good reason; others suffered from what could only be called a "bad press." Identify the names and explain why each has a special entry in the annals of infamy.

1. Adrien Arcand.
2. François Bigot.
3. Charles Lawrence.
4. Robert Stobo.
5. Louis-Joseph Papineau.
6. John Strachan.
7. Lord Durham.
8. Louis Riel.
9. Sir Joseph Flavelle.
10. R.B. Bennett.
11. Fred Rose.
12. Paul Rose.
13. Clifford Olson.

---

64. Brave Men and Women

In defense of their ideals, the men and women of Canada have shown signal courage, resolution, and bravery. Not all of them have their deeds described in history books. See if you can match the deed with the name.

1. He shot down seventy-two enemy planes and was the first Canadian airman to be awarded the Victoria Cross.

2. After a resounding victory at Detroit, he died on the slopes of Queenston Heights, and his fame grew larger in death than in life.

3. With sixteen volunteers and forty-two loyal Indians, he held off the Iroquois, and may well have saved the colony of New France.

4. To warn the British that the American troops were approaching, she treked through the woods at night, with or without a cow.

5. He was a piper and he piped the men of his country over the top of the Regina Trench at the Battle of the Somme, 8 October 1916, and was awarded the Victoria Cross posthumously.

6. A cavalry commander, he won a major victory at Duck Lake, lost one at Batoche, where he died twenty-one years later.

7. This pilot officer remained in the burning Lancaster bomber, struggling to rescue the rear-gunner (who survived though the pilot officer did not).

A. Gabriel Dumont.

B. Andrew Mynarski.

C. James C. Richardson

D. Adam Dollard.

E. Sir Isaac Brock.

F. Billy Bishop.

G. Laura Secord.

---

65. Love Stories

The history of this country is not lacking in great love stories. The problem is that most — if not all — are sad (even tragic) romances. Here are five romances. Can you answer the questions?

1. She accompanied a relative, Sieur de Roberval, on his voyage to colonize New France in 1542. When Roberval discovered that her lover was also on board he abandoned her on the wilds of Ile des Démons in the Gulf of St. Lawrence. She was joined by her lover, where she gave birth to their child. Then the child died, the lover died, and she would have succumbed, had not fishermen rescued her two years after the abandonment. What is the name of this unfortunate woman?

2. She was parted from her lover and it was not until years later that her search ended. She found him again, but he was engaged to be married to another woman. She died of shock. The incident so inspired a poet that ninety-two years after the incident he published a narrative poem. The poem inspired Philippe and Henri Hébert's bronze statue of the woman and her tragic memory. What was her name?

3. She was Madame de St. Laurent, and he was Edward Augustus, Duke of Kent, Commander in Chief of British North America. Their liaison in Halifax and Quebec City lasted twenty-seven years and produced two sons. He described his precious Julie in a letter: "She is of very good family and has never been an actress." She entered a convent for the rest of her life when he was summoned back to England. His subsequent marriage resulted in one child, a daughter. What was her name?

4. She was the daughter of a famous novelist. She fell madly in love with Albert Pinson, a British naval officer, who failed to return her affections. When he was stationed in Halifax, she lived there as "Miss Lewly" from 1863 to 1864. She gradually lapsed into insanity. François Truffaut based a film on her life in 1975. What was her name, and what was the name of the film?

5. She was a carefree young woman from British Columbia, and he was an older and more thoughtful bachelor from Montreal. Their romance was kept secret but their wedding made world headlines. Their relationship produced three sons before it disintegrated, with the former lovers going their separate ways. Who are they? What are the names of their sons?

66. Mottoes and Slogans

Almost every newspaper and magazine in the country has its own motto or slogan. Here is a list of publications to match up with a list of phrases.

1. *The Canadian Forum.*	**A.** "On the Level."
2. *The Globe and Mail.*	**B.** "Reach for the Star — Most People Do."
3. *Maclean's.*	**C.** "Freedom of Trade, Liberty of Religion, Equality of Civil Rights."
4. *The Northern Miner.*	**D.** "Canada's Weekly Newsmagazine."
5. *La Presse.*	**E.** "Canada's National Newspaper."
6. *The Toronto Star.*	**F.** "An Independent Journal of Opinion and the Arts."
7. *The Winnipeg Free Press.*	**G.** "That's My Kind of Paper."
8. *The Winnipeg Tribune.*	**H.** "North America's Largest French-language Daily."

67. Newspapering People

A newspaper to be outstanding requires a publisher or editor who is also outstanding. There appears below a list of some of the country's outstanding newspapering personalities. Some made names for themselves and their papers through acquisition, through founding, or through editing, writing, or commenting. Match the personality with the achievement to complete the sentence.

1. Lord Atholstan   **A.** was a nationalist, a Member of Parliament, and a founder of *Le Devoir* in 1910.

66

2. Joseph E. Atkinson   **B.** was successively editor of the *Winnipeg Free Press*, the *Victoria Times*, and the *Vancouver Sun*.

3. Lord Beaverbrook   **C.** is nationally known as a novelist but in the 1970s edited *La Presse*.

4. Henri Bourassa   **D.** was influential as editor of the *Ottawa Journal*, then as Royal Commissioner and as Senator.

5. George Brown   **E.** was called "the tribune of Nova Scotia" and was the editor of the *Novascotian*.

6. John W. Dafoe   **F.** was known as "Holy Joe" for his social views while publisher of the *Toronto Star*.

7. Robert (Bob) Edwards   **G.** was born Hugh Graham and was the founder publisher of the *Montreal Star* in 1867.

8. Joseph Howe   **H.** began publishing the *Colonial Advocate* and then took part in the Rebellion of 1837.

9. Bruce Hutchison   **I.** was a Minister of the Interior and then owner of the *Winnipeg Free Press*.

10. Roger Lemelin   **J.** was the founder of *The Globe*, a Father of Confederation, and a Senator before being assassinated.

11. George McCullagh   **K.** was an Imperialist who controlled the *Daily Express*, the *Sunday Express*, and the *Evening Standard*.

12. W.L. Mackenzie   **L.** was the satirist who published in 1902-22 the *Eye Opener*.

13. Margaret (Ma) Murray   **M.** amalgamated two papers in 1936 to create the *Globe and Mail*.

14. Grattan O'Leary   **N.** was the leading editor of the day who enjoyed long association with the *Winnipeg Free Press*.

15. Sir Clifford Sifton   **O.** was the outspoken publisher of both *The Alaska Highway News* and then the *Bridge-River Lillooet News*.

16. Roy Thomson   **P.** a genuine press baron since 1964, his holdings included *The Times*.

---

68. Bits and Pieces

"A journalist is hardly an authority upon anything — unless perhaps upon the appraisal of the drift of public opinion," wrote John W. Dafoe, editor of the *Winnipeg Free Press*. Here are questions concerned with journalistic matters that should be part of public information, if not public opinion.

1. What is the name of the most widely sold magazine in Canada, over 900,000 copies of which appear each week in twelve regional editions?

2. Who is the Vancouver-based columnist whose irreverent views and baroque style have earned him the sobriquet "The Wicked Wit of the West"?

3. The first newspaper that was published in what is now Canada appeared on 23 March 1752. It was issued by John Bushell, and its title was *The _____ Gazette*.

4. There is a French-language edition of *Maclean's*. What is it called?

5. Milt Dunnell, Scott Young, Dick Beddoes, Jim Proudfoot, Ted Reeve, Jim Vipond, and Christie Blatchford have all made names for themselves as _____ reporters.

6. The *Globe and Mail*, owned by Thomson, is Canada's largest-circulation newspaper. True of false.

7. The *Canadian Jewish Chronicle Review*, founded in Toronto in 1921, was published there until 1930, when it was published from Montreal. Why was the editorial office moved?

8. It is the only daily Canadian newspaper sold in the Soviet Union, and it is the only one to maintain a bureau in Peking. Name the paper.

9. What is *TV Guide* called in French?

10. Here are the names of seven syndicated, or once-syndicated, columnists. Unfortunately in transmission, the first and last names were transposed. Wield the blue pencil and correct them.
    A. Allan Lynch.
    B. Charles Stevens.
    C. Dalton Fraser.
    D. John Gwyn.
    E. Peter Fotheringham.
    F. Richard Camp.
    G. Geoffrey Newman.

11. Which is the largest, French-language daily newspaper, *Le Devoir* or *La Presse*?

12. Name the important drama critic who was once the whole reporting staff and factotum of the pro-labor paper, the *Glace Bay Gazette*.

13. Name the writer of "News from Old Crow" whose catch-phrase "Here are the News" became the title of her autobiography.

14. Is the *Calgary Herald* owned by Southam Press Limited or by FP Publications Limited?

15. Which of the four chains — Southam Press Limited, Thomson Newspapers Ltd., FP Publications Limited, and Québécor Inc. — has the largest holdings in small daily and weekly newspapers?

16. What does "CP" signify at the head of a story? What does (or did, as the custom is dying out) "—30—" signify at the end of a story?

LANGUAGE

69. Differences in English

Winston Churchill once quipped that the English-speaking people are divided by a common tongue. Certainly there are noticeable differences between the English spoken in Great Britain and the English spoken in North America. This is particularly so in terms of vocabulary, as the following lists demonstrate. On the left are words common in Canada and the United States; on the right, words common in Great Britain. Of these common words, the last nine refer to automobiles. Fill in the blanks.

North America	Great Britain
1. Apartment.	A.
2.	B. Sweets.
3. Flashlight.	C.
4. Sidewalk.	D.
5.	E. Paraffin.
6. Roomer.	F.
7. Fender.	G.
8. Generator.	H.
9.	I. Bonnet.
10.	J. Spanner.
11. Muffler.	K.
12. Truck.	L.
13. Highway.	M.
14.	N. Road diversion.
15. Gas station.	O.

70. Languages: Official and Unofficial

A goodly number of Canadians speak the "unofficial languages" — that is, languages other than the two "official languages," English and French. How knowledgeable are you about the languages spoken by Canadians? Answer these questions and find out.

1. More Canadians speak Ukrainian than Italian. True or false.
2. About as many Canadians speak Russian as do Welsh. True or false.
3. After English and French, German is spoken by more Canadians than any other language. True or false.
4. The Indians speak a dozen different languages, like Algonkian and Wakashan, but the Inuit speak a single language. What is its name?
5. Polish and Dutch are spoken by, roughly, the same number of people. True or false.
6. More Canadians speak English with a Scottish accent than with an Irish accent. True or false.
7. In the 1970s, English was the mother tongue of approximately 13 million, French of approximately 6 million. True or false.

LAW

71. Historic Acts

This quiz tries your knowledge of some legal measures in Canada's past and present. These are milestones — stepping stones in the development of the country. The reports, decisions, treaties, acts, etc., are listed on the left along with the dates they were signed. On the right appear summary statements of what they accomplished. Match them up.

1. The Treaty of Utrecht, 11 April 1713.

2. The Treaty of Paris, 10 February 1763.

3. The Quebec Act, 22 June 1774.

4. The Constitutional Act, 26 December 1791.

5. The Treaty of Ghent, 24 December 1814.

6. The Act of Union, 10 February 1841.

7. The British North America Act, 29 March 1867.

8. The "Persons" Case Decision, 18 October 1929.

A. Great Britain and the United States formally end the War of 1812.

B. The Imperial Conference adopts the resolution that the Dominions are "autonomous communities . . . equal in status."

C. Royal assent given to legislative union of New Brunswick, Nova Scotia, and Canada (East and West).

D. The British Parliament formally recognizes the status of the British Dominions.

E. France cedes to Great Britain all possessions in northern North America except for St. Pierre and Miquelon.

F. The British Privy Council declares women to be "persons" within the meaning of the BNA Act.

G. Great Britain and France agree to cede Acadia and Newfoundland to the English.

H. New boundaries are established for Quebec as well as a legal system partly British and partly French.

9. The Balfour Report,
18 November 1926.

10. The Statute of Westminster,
12 December 1931.

11. The Canadian Citizenship
Act, 1 July 1946.

12. The Canada Constitution Act,
29 March 1982.

I. Parliament proclaims an act providing
for the creation of a Canadian citizen
to take effect 1 January 1947.

J. Royal assent given to Bill 43 to
"patriate the Constitution" and to
create the Canadian Charter of Rights
and Freedoms.

K. Upper Canada and Lower Canada are
united in the Province of Canada.

L. Quebec is divided into Upper Canada
and Lower Canada.

---

72. Criminals

This quiz is based on relating criminals and crimes. It should be noted that although society and the courts judged these men and women guilty of their crimes, some were not criminals in the usual sense of the word, but were people of principle with causes of their own. Some were high-minded; others, bloody-minded. Match the man or woman with his or her deed, paying particular attention to the all-important date.

1. Almighty Voice,
30 May 1897.

2. Edwin Alonzo Boyd,
8 September 1952.

3. Marie-Josephte Corriveau,
15 April 1763.

4. Peter Demeter,
4 December 1974.

5. Evelyn Dick,
6 March 1946.

6. Albert-Joseph Guay,
9 September 1949.

7. Simon Gun-an-noot,
24 June 1919.

8. Albert Johnson,
17 February 1932.

A. The bomb he planted aboard the CP
DC-3 exploded, killing everyone
aboard, including his wife.

B. After years on the run, this fugitive
wanted for murder surrendered at
Hazelton, B.C.

C. Using as an excuse he was flooding
the rink (in above-zero weather), the
prisoner made his celebrated escape
from Bordeaux Jail.

D. He was, after a sensational trial,
found guilty and on this day hanged
for poisoning his wife.

E. A shootout in the Yukon ended a
massive manhunt for the man who
murdered prospectors for the gold in
their teeth.

F. He fell in a hail of bullets while trying
to rob a bank. He was a "reformed"
and paroled thief.

G. On this day she killed her husband
whose torso was found in the
Hamilton Escarpment. Then the body
of her infant son was found encased
in cement in a suitcase in the attic.

H. A shootout in a poplar bluff ended an
epic two-year manhunt in the North
West, following the killing of a
Mountie.

9. Dr. William Henry King,
   9 June 1859.

10. Donald Morrison, 1888-90.

11. Lucien Rivard,
    2 March 1965.

12. Norman (Red) Ryan,
    25 May 1936.

I. For the murder of her husband, she
    was hanged at Quebec; her body was
    exposed in an iron cage for a month.
J. Killing an inspector who attempted to
    arrest him for suspected arson, he
    eluded arrest for two years with the
    help of his Megantic County friends.
K. He led members of his gang in a
    daring escape from Toronto's Don
    Jail and sparked the greatest
    manhunt in Canadian history.
L. After the longest trial in Canadian
    history he was found guilty of
    arranging "by person or persons
    unknown" the slaying of his wife.

73. Identify That Verse

The subject is Canadian verse; the task is to identify the poet and, if possible, the poem. The lines below were written by major Canadian poets and they come from fine poems. See if you can identify them.

1. Along the line of smoky hills
     The crimson forest stands,
   And all the day the blue-jay calls
     Throughout the autumn lands.

2. Be strong, O paddle! be brave, canoe!
   The reckless waves you must plunge into.
   Reel, reel,
   On your trembling keel,
   But never a fear my craft will feel.

3. Take up our quarrel with the foe:
   To you from failing hands we throw
     The torch; be yours to hold it high.
     If ye break faith with us who die
   We shall not sleep. . . .

4. Were you ever out in the Great Alone, when the moon was
     awful clear,
   And the icy mountains hemmed you in with a silence you most
     could *hear*;
   With only the howl of a timber wolf, and you camped there in
     the cold. . . .

5. Hidden in wonder and snow, or sudden with summer,
   The land stares at the sun in a huge silence
   Endlessly repeating something we cannot hear.
   Inarticulate, arctic. . . .

6. This is a beauty
   of dissonance,
   this resonance
   of stony strand,
   this smoky cry
   curled over a black pine. . . .

7. I said that he fell straight to the ice where they found him.
   And none but the sun and incurious clouds have lingered
   Around the marks of that day on the ledge of the Finger,
   That day, the last of my youth, on the last of our mountains.

8. And me happiest when I compose poems.
     Love, power, the huzza of battle
     are something, are much;
   yet a poem includes them like a pool
     water and reflection.

---

74. Top Ten Novels

A list of the hundred "most significant" Canadian novels was drawn up by professors of English meeting at the University of Calgary in April 1978. The list may not have been complete (inexplicably it omitted any of the novels of Hugh Garner) but it did act as a guide to what was being read (and taught) in the 1970s. Here are clues to the top ten novels and their authors. Are these "the best"? How many have you read?

1. A heavenly being made of rock by a Margaret whose name resembles that of a river.
2. Activity, neither third nor fourth, associated with the theatre by a former newspaper editor and publisher.
3. As for this author and his novel, he talks about himself and his dwelling and his first name rhymes with Lake St. Clair.
4. Concerned with the hills and dales of human experience by an earnest man who buckles down.
5. A wind instrument supplies the title for this novel by the novelist whose last name resembles king in another language.
6. This novel could be seen as the Canadian version of *What Makes Sammy Run* by a writer whose last name begins with four letters suggestive of wealth.
7. Twin or two should grab you with this work by an author whose name recalls that of Sherlock Holmes's sidekick.
8. A biblical quotation entitles this novel, written by (if you associate) hue, buddy, Beatle.
9. The Bible again asks the question of the title and the answer is a breezy one by the writer whose first two initials are what you say to a horse and whose last name ends in the letters for the inferno.
10. The list was begun by the Margaret who ends it, but the novel is different for this one is composed of the definite article plus those who discover by means of a rod.

---

75. Novel Beginnings

Novelists begin their novels in characteristic ways. Who will ever forget the opening of Tolstoy's *Anna Karenina*? "All happy families resemble each other, each unhappy family is unhappy in its own way." What follow are the opening sentences of twelve novels (on the left), and the names of twelve novels and their authors (on the right). Match them up, if you can.

1. "There are some stories into which the reader should be led gently, and I think this may be one of them."

2. "Here was the least common denominator of nature, the skeleton requirements simply, of land and sky — Saskatchewan prairie."

3. "What with his wife so ill these past few weeks and the prospect of three more days of teaching before the weekend break, Mr. MacPherson felt unusually glum."

4. "I don't know whether you know Mariposa."

5. "My lifelong involvement with Mrs. Dempster began at 5:58 o'clock p.m. on the 27th of December, 1908, at which time I was ten years and seven months old."

6. "Where was the young man who had given her so many admiring glances yesterday?"

7. "David Canaan had lived in Entremont all his thirty years."

8. "Senator Maclean, the investment banker and mining magnate, watched at the window for hours for the car to come down the road from the prison."

9. "Greta was at the stove."

10. "Philip has thrown himself across the bed and fallen asleep, his clothes on still, one of his long legs dangling to the floor."

11. "They are, I thought sadly, what they eat."

12. "The river flowed both ways."

A. *The Mountain and the Valley* by Ernest Buckler.

B. *More Joy in Heaven* by Morley Callaghan.

C. *Fifth Business* by Robertson Davies.

D. *The Diviners* by Margaret Laurence.

E. *Sunshine Sketches of a Little Town* by Stephen Leacock.

F. *The Watch that Ends the Night* by Hugh MacLennan

G. *General Ludd* by John Metcalf.

H. *Who Has Seen the Wind?* by W.O. Mitchell.

I. *The Apprenticeship of Duddy Kravitz* by Mordecai Richler.

J. *As for Me and My House* by Sinclair Ross.

K. *The Tin Flute* by Gabrielle Roy.

L. *The Double Hook* by Sheila Watson.

112. New Place Names

Some places in the country boast not one but two names — one old and one new. The varied questions in this set test your knowledge of those places that have changed their names, and of those few that have strenuously and successfully resisted the pressures to do so. How good is your memory? Answer these questions to find out.

1. Assiniboia became, in 1870, part of the newly formed Province of _____.
2. During the First World War, in southern Ontario, townsfolk voted to change their town's name. Five names appeared on the ballot: Adanac, Benton, Brock, Corona, and Kitchener. Which name received the greatest number of votes and so became the name of the town? What was the town formerly called?
3. It was originally called Ile Royale, it now prides itself on being more Scots than Scotland. What is it called today? It was originally called Ile Saint-Jean, it now boasts of being a "million-acre farm." What is it called today?
4. Stadacona and Hochelaga were Iroquois settlements visited by Jacques Cartier in 1535. What modern cities stand on these sites today?
5. Two towns at the head of Lake Superior amalgamated in 1970. Name the two towns. Give the present name of the twin cities.
6. Read the following description, then answer the questions that follow: "In the pre-settlement era, the area had been a favoured buffalo-hunting ground for the Indian and the Métis. The herds were run into pounds constructed along the creek. Bone piles, accumulated from the frequent slaughters, gave the creek its name, which in Cree is Oskana or Wascana."
   A. What is the meaning of Wascana?
   B. What city is being discussed?
   (Clue: The site acquired its present name in 1882, and it is a provincial capital.)
7. Kenora, on Lake of the Woods, was so named in 1905. It was named after:
   A. The Cree word for "ford" or "watery passageway."
   B. The initial letters of Keewatin, Norman, and Rat Portage.
   C. Joseph Kenora, a local prospector and city father.
8. In the 17th century it was a Senecan village known as Teiaiagon; in the 18th century, a French post named Fort Rouillé; in the 19th century, an English town known as York. In 1834, it became _____.

---

113. Scrambled Place Names

How quickly are you able to unscramble the place names that follow? To give this quiz a geographical turn, the nine names in Part One are of places in the West, and the nine names in Part Two are of places in the East.

Part One
1. Lalebocoal.
2. Langer.
3. Nekawol.
4. Motdonne.
5. Mashquis.
6. Pinewing.
7. Polosmak.
8. Soonatask.
9. Senlon.

Part Two
1. Danger.
2. Drop It Net.
3. I Ate Card.
4. O Scan.
5. Of Lands I Go.
6. No Real Mt.
7. Rare Bacon.
8. Torn Too.
9. Say Other.

---

114. Famous Sights

It should be neither too difficult nor too easy to identify all of these famous or familiar sights. All ten provinces are represented in this selection of thirteen photographs. The photos appear in no particular order. See if you can identify the sight and name the province in which it is found.

1.

2.

3.

4.

5.

6.

7.

8.

9.

10.

11.

12.

13.

115. States and Provinces

These questions may be answered in one of two ways. Answer them without looking at a map, or answer them after looking at a map. In fact, it might be fun to answer them twice — the first time without a map, the second time with a map of North America. Then there is no need to check the answers at the back of the book! Are the following statements true or false?

1. British Columbia touches both Alaska and Idaho.   T   F
2. Alberta touches both Idaho and Montana.   T   F
3. Saskatchewan touches both Montana and North Dakota.   T   F
4. Manitoba touches both North Dakota and Minnesota.   T   F
5. Ontario touches both Wisconsin and Pennsylvania.   T   F
6. Quebec touches both New York State and Massachusetts.   T   F
7. New Brunswick touches both Maine and New Hampshire.   T   F
8. Nova Scotia touches both New Brunswick and Maine.   T   F

---

116. Holiday Fun in Eastern Canada

Visit the tourist sights in Eastern Canada — by plane, car, train, or bus. These are among the sights you will want to see. To find out the name of the places they are located, fill in the blanks.

1. Built by the French in 1713, leveled by the English in 1758, this French fortified town, which once sheltered five thousand people, has been under continuous reconstruction since 1961. It is the largest fort in North America and well worth a visit. But you will have to go to _____, N.S., to find it.

2. Be certain, when traveling through northern Ontario, to watch out for the Giant Goose. This 9 metre- (30-foot-) long steel sculpture of a wild goose in flight may be seen from the highway outside _____, Ont.

3. Santa's Village, near _____, Ont., may be visited year-round. It is situated in the vacation land of Muskoka, where there is swimming in the summer and skiing in the winter. Close by there is a small Dinosaur Park with life-size models of these prehistoric beasts.

4. Be among the three million tourists who annually visit St. Joseph's Oratory. While in the same city, shop underground in Place Ville Marie, tour historic churches, attend a game at the Olympic Stadium and a concert at Place des Arts, in the world's second-largest French city, _____, Que.

5. The southernmost tip of the Canadian mainland has the same latitude as northern California, Ankara, and Rome. It has the climate to prove it, for at _____, Ont., there is a national park with a 14.5-kilometre- (9-mile-) long sandy peninsula. In the park one may see a great profusion of flowers plus a great variety of birds (over 300 species have been spotted).

6. Citadel Hill, with its Old Town Clock (dating from 1803), is but one of the many historic attractions of _____, N.S. While here, be certain to see Bedford Basin and Province House (with its fine Georgian architecture).

7. Visit historic _____, Que., where there stands the Château Frontenac, the Wolfe-Montcalm Monument, Dufferin Terrace, etc. Go in February and attend the Winter Carnival. That 2.13 metre (7-foot) snowman is Bonhomme Carnaval.

8. There are gannets galore in this famous bird sanctuary. It was first visited by Champlain who described its most characteristic feature — an immense limestone rock, 18 metres (60 feet) high, 30.5 metres (100 feet) wide, pierced by a natural arch. He gave the rock its present name. The place to be is _____, Que.

9. What is the name of one of the famous scenic drives in North America? This 296 kilometre (184-mile) trail skirts the rugged coastline of the northern half of Cape Breton Island, N.S., offering travelers vistas of sea and highland, plus excursions to Baddeck (where Alexander Graham Bell lived), beautiful Bras d'Or Lakes, and Louisbourg. The _____ Trail was named after the explorer _____.

10. Visit the world's longest covered bridge when traveling in New Brunswick. The bridge crosses the Saint John River at _____.

11. When you visit _____, Ont., be on the lookout for the "biggest moose in the world." Outside the tourist bureau stands the 5.48-metre (18-foot) steel and concrete bull moose, said to be the world's biggest.

---

117. Holiday Fun in Western Canada

If you want some more fun, visit the tourist sights in Western Canada. But to do so, you will have to know where to go — by bus, train, car, or plane. Here are some of the sights you will want to see. All you need to know is the places they are located. To find that out, fill in the blanks.

1. One of its kind and not to be missed is the Nikka Yuko Centennial Garden. It was built in 1967 by the citizens of this city and the six thousand Japanese who were settled here in 1941. Kimono-clad geishas serve tea, and tourists will marvel at the small island in the pool which has been given the shape of a turtle. The Garden is located in _____, Alta.

2. Visit Lost Lagoon, Prospect Point, Siwash Rock, the cricket fields of Brockton Point, the Nine O'Clock Gun, plus the Aquarium and much more in Stanley Park. It is the pride of _____, B.C.

3. The thing to do when you pass through _____, Alta., is to be certain to view the giant Easter Egg. It is made of steel and decorated with traditional Ukrainian colors and designs.

4. In _____, Alta., you can climb the 191-metre- (626-foot-) high tower, troop through the Glenbow-Alberta Institute, where you admire the art and artifacts, attend the Stampede (in July), visit the Horseman's Hall of Fame, and watch the fish hatch at the Trout Hatchery.

5. Visit Robert Service's Cabin (the very one in which he wrote his verse "The Shooting of Dan McGrew"), trek out to the Chilkoot Pass, examine the sternwheeler *Klondike*, and attend the Polar Games which are held annually for children. Do this in _____, Y.T.

6. The oldest of the national parks is worth a long visit, for it has two fine resorts. There are snowcapped peaks to ski, deep crystal-clear lakes in which to swim, hot mineral springs in which to bathe, even a school of fine arts to attend. The place to go is _____, Alta.

7. Dinosaurs are terrifying even in fossil form. You can see the fossils at Dinosaur Provincial Park, about 48 kilometres (30 miles) from Brooks, Alta., in the middle of the _____. For sculptor John Kanerva's life-size replicas of the thunderous lizards, visit the Natural History Park in Calgary, Alta.

8. For a boom town that went bust and then had the good fortune to be revived, visit the "gold rush capital of the Cariboo." The reconstructed town of _____, B.C., is a living museum. There is a registry office, a hotel, even a saloon (Wake Up Jake Saloon).

9. Travel even further into the past when you visit 'Ksan, the replica of a Gitksan Indian village as it was before the advent of the Europeans. Traditional arts and crafts flourish here, along with longhouses, totem poles, canoes, even a Feast House and a Treasure House. But to go to 'Ksan, you must first travel to _____, B.C.

10. When in _____, Man., be sure to see the replica of the *Nonsuch*, built by the Hudson's Bay Company to celebrate its three hundredth anniversary.

11. Where else but in _____, Sask., can you see the Wascana Center, scenic and cultural center of the city, as well as the training school of the RCMP?

118. National Parks

This is a country of the great outdoors, at least as far as the people at Parks Canada are concerned. Through five regional offices, Parks Canada manages twenty-eight National Parks covering more than 50,000 square miles. How many of these parklands have you visited? Under each province are listed two National Parks — one of which will be found in that province, the other being a completely fictitious park. Identify the real parks in the right provinces.

1. In British Columbia you will find:
   A. Cariboo National Park.
   B. Yoho National Park.

2. In Alberta you will find:
   A. Banff National Park.
   B. Rocky Mountain National Park.

3. In Saskatchewan you will find:
   A. Batoche National Park.
   B. Prince Albert National Park.

4. In Manitoba you will find:
   A. Norquay National Park.
   B. Riding Mountain National Park.

5. In Ontario you will find:
   A. Muskoka National Park.
   B. Pukaskwa National Park.

6. In Quebec you will find:
   A. Brébeuf National Park.
   B. Forillon National Park.

7. In New Brunswick you will find:
   A. Kouchibouguac National Park.
   B. Nowlan National Park.

8. In Nova Scotia you will find:
   A. Bedford Basin National Park.
   B. Kejimkujik National Park.
9. In Prince Edward Island you will find:
   A. Green Gables National Park.
   B. Prince Edward Island National Park.
10. In Newfoundland you will find:
    A. Gros Morne National Park.
    B. Mowat National Park.
11. In the Northwest Territories you will find:
    A. Baffin Island National Park.
    B. Wood Buffalo National Park.
12. In the Yukon Territory you will find:
    A. Klondike National Park.
    B. Kluane National Park.

119. Provincial Parks

In addition to the National Park system, there are parks of all sizes
maintained by the provincial governments. There are over one thousand of
these parks. This quiz is based on placing these parks in their proper
provinces, based on a knowledge of topography and history.

1. Blow Me Down (Lark Harbour) and Sir Richard Squires Memorial Park are
   provincial parks in _____.
2. Chibaugamau and Mont Tremblant are provincial parks in _____.
3. Asessippi and Turtle Mountain are provincial parks in _____.
4. Campbell's Cove and Jacques Cartier are provincial parks in _____.
5. Algonquin and Quetico are provincial parks in _____.
6. Crooked River and Garibaldi are provincial parks in _____.
7. Whycocomagh and Five Islands are provincial parks in _____.
8. Cypress Hills and Lac La Ronge are provincial parks in _____.
9. Bow Valley and Writing-on-Stone are provincial parks in _____.
10. Mactaquac and New River Beach are provincial parks in _____.

120. Notable Regions

Canada is a country of pronounced regions, each with its own topography
and traditions. Locate the following regions in their provinces, or identify
regions when their provinces are given.

1. Straddling the border between southern Saskatchewan and Alberta is a hilly
   region, some 137 metres (450 feet) above sea level, with fossil and other
   remains. What is this rolling region called?
2. South of the St. Lawrence and east of the Richelieu is a region renowned
   for its rural charm. The Loyalists loved this garden-like setting, as do
   vacationers today. Name the townships and the province they are in.

3. This fruit-growing valley has a salubrious climate and is a favorite vacation area, drawing visitors for thousands of kilometres. The lake has its own sea serpent, the natives say. What is the area called and what province may it be found in?

4. Torontonians flock to this region of lakes and rivers for the fishing and swimming, and in the winter for the skiing and hunting. Sometimes called "cottage country," it has a better (and Indian) name. What is it?

5. This river valley was opened up for its lumber, and now it attracts vacationers who enjoy its rural charms and folksingers who attend an annual summer festival of music. It is no secret the valley is named after the river which empties into the Gulf of St. Lawrence. Name the valley.

6. Here is another valley, this one with a long tradition of Anglo-Saxon settlement and lumbering aplenty. The river in question flows into the St. Lawrence at Montreal. Inhabitants of the area speak with a special "accent." What is the area? What is the province?

7. Prospectors greeted ranchers, Indians greeted whites, in this rugged country, somewhat isolated then as now in the interior of British Columbia. Mountains, road, deer, and Eskimo share this name. Give its name.

8. In western Nova Scotia, famed for its association with the Acadians, lies a wonderful valley. Its scenic attractions are well known, and it is a relatively prosperous mixed farming region widely known for its delicious apples. What is the valley called?

9. This playground area is shared with the United States. It is mainly islands, rocky islands, in the St. Lawrence River. Some are populated year-round. Others are too small to be useful except to be scenic. There is a castle on one of them. The climate is especially pleasant, and there is even a tower from which one may view the playground. Which province? What region?

QUOTATIONS

121. Who Said That?

Memorable remarks are those that appeal to the imagination and the memory and are recalled years after they were originally made. Below appear eight memorable remarks made by Canadians. Which Canadians?

1. "Living next to you is in some ways like sleeping with an elephant."
2. "My place is marching with the workers rather than riding with General Motors."
3. "Kemo Sabe."
4. "What's a million?"
5. "The Montreal Olympics can no more have a deficit than a man can have a baby."
6. "We live in a fire-proof house, far from inflammable materials."
7. "A television franchise is a license to print money."
8. "Fuddle duddle."

122. Mystery Quotations

This series of puzzles requires the reader to reveal the mystery quotation in each maze of letters. The quotation is a familiar phrase or sentence associated with Canadian history or nationalism. Begin with the letter indicated and advance from letter to letter until the final letter has been reached. Move left or right, up or down, but never diagonally. A letter is used once only.

1. Begin with F.

```
M   O   R   F

S   T   O   S

E   A   A   E
```

2. Begin with T (in upper left).

```
T   T   R   N   O

H   E   U   E   R

R   F   N   O   T

E   D   G   R   H

E   N   A   T   S
```

3. Begin with A (the one on the lower right).

```
T   S   I   Y   A   S

H   B   E   E   N   N

A   S   E   V   D   A

T   A   R   E   O   C

T   H   Y   N   N   I

H   K   W   I   E   L

E   R   A   L   W   L

W   O   Y   L   E   A
```

4. Begin with J (for a French quotation).

```
U   V   I   E

O   M   E   N

S   E   J   S
```

5. Begin with the V on the third line (for a French declaration).

```
E  R  B
C  L  I
E  !  V
B  V  I
E  E  L
U  Q  E
```

6. Begin with T (upper right).

```
A  Y  T
L  E  H
W  A  Y
E  G  S
T  R  M
T  I  A
H  E  N
```

7. Begin with an H.

```
S  H  S  H
E  E  T  E
R  S  O  S
O  C  O  H
```

8. Begin with the middle T.

```
E  M  E
D  E  G
I  H  A
U  T  S
M  E  S
I  M  E
S  T  H
```

9. Begin with the L (left-hand column).

```
S   G   E   L
L   U   N   G
K   C   O   L
I   S   A   N
E   B   H   T
T   T   E   R
```

10. Just begin!

```
E   P
H   O
F   O
O   N
H   T
R   A
A   M
```

RADIO

123. Broadcasting

"If we fail to communicate," noted veteran broadcaster Robert Weaver, "the country will fall into parishes." Radio broadcasting was for decades the principal means of national communication, and alongside television broadcasting it remains an important medium of expression. Here are some questions on Canadian radio.

1. XWA were the call letters of Canada's first radio station, licensed to broadcast in 1919. The station, run by Marconi, was located in the city of _____. It transmitted the first scheduled broadcast in North America on 20 May 1920. The letter "X" stood for "experimental." The station is currently in operation as _____.

2. The immediate forerunner of the Canadian Broadcasting Corporation was the C_____ R_____ B_____ C_____, which supervised all private and public broadcasting until the creation of the CBC.

3. The first series of radio dramas produced in Canada was called "The _____ of _____" series. This weekly series of sixty-minute programs, dramatized events in early Canadian history, was produced live in _____ each week by the CRBC. The series was launched in 1931 with a program on the last voyage of Henry _____. The series was written by Merrill _____ and directed by Tyrone _____.

4. The Moose River Mining Disaster occurred on 12 April 1936, imprisoning three men. Rather than issue bulletins from the radio studio in _____, a young announcer traveled to the mine site and broadcast from there, thereby creating Canada's first actuality coverage. For sixty-nine hours he reported on the progress of rescue operations. All three men were rescued. The announcer emerged with a national reputation. His name is _____.

5. The Canadian Broadcasting Corporation, which was created on 2 Nov. 1936, is the world's largest broadcasting system. True or false.

6. Older than the CBC is CFRB, which was started in Toronto in 1927 by E. S. (Ted) Rogers who developed the alternating-current radio tube, which made

modern broadcasting possible. The station enjoys the largest audience in Canada. Its call letters are significant. CF is the once-standard prefix for "Canada". RB stands for _____.

7. A well-known sports broadcaster owns the Toronto FM station CKFH. In fact, his initials appear in the call letters. Who is the owner?

8. The fact that Canada has a mix of private and public broadcasting is attributable to the efforts of the C_____ R_____ L _____, which was founded as a lobby by Alan B. P_____ and Graham S_____.

9. The CBC, in the 1940s and 1950s, had two national radio networks. The first was known as the T_____ C_____ Network; the second, the D_____ Network. They were consolidated into the CBC R_____ Network in 1962.

10. What is the foreign service of CBC Radio called?

11. In the 1970s, Canada acquired the CKO network. What is unique about the programming of this network?

12. GRS is the abbreviation of General Radio Service, authorized by the Department of Communications in April 1962. It makes available the 27 megahertz band. What is its popular name?

---

124. Anyone Listening?

Anyone who has listened for any length of time to radio in Canada should be able to answer the majority of the questions that follow, all of which deal with popular, or once-popular, radio personalities and programs. Answer the questions, or fill in the blanks.

1. The "Wayne and Shuster Show" features Johnny Wayne and Frank Shuster. Which is the short one?

2. Frank Deaville and Art McGregor teamed up to create the comedy team popular in the 1930s and 1940s. It was known as _____.

3. Forties radio was a good time for Mrs. A. Who was she?

4. Between 1944 and 1953, Andrew Allan produced an impressive CBC dramatic series. What was it called?

5. What was the name of the popular children's character created by Mary Grannan for CBC Radio between 1947 and 1954?

6. Old Rawhide is a character with a sarcastic wit created and impersonated by veteran broadcaster _____.

7. What have Charles Jennings, Lorne Greene, Frank Herbert, and Earl Cameron in common?

8. A series of important educational programs was co-produced by the CBC and the Canadian Association for Adult Education. The programs established "listening groups" across the country. What were the programs called?

9. Neil LeRoy moderated a popular CBC show from 1946 to 1968 in which panelists reached verdicts on controversial questions submitted by listeners. What was the show called?

10. Bill McNeil and Maria Barrett were identified with what popular program?

11. BF and AM are the initials of former interviewers on "As It Happens." What are their names?

12. What popular weekly morning program has been hosted by the following broadcasters: Michael Enright, Peter Gzowski, Bruno Gerussi, and Don Harron?
13. What is the French name of the CBC?
14. A number of people have been dubbed "Mr. Canada," but one of them earned the title — for his breathless broadcasts on colorful Canada. Who was he?

125. Quiz Programs

Any self-respecting Canadiana quiz book should devote a set of questions to the Canadian achievement in quiz programs. What we have here is a set of questions about radio quiz shows of the past and present. Excluded are audience-participation "giveaway" shows.

1. "King of Quizz" is the title he gave himself. He persisted in spelling the word with two z's — like "jazz" and "fuzz" — and he claimed he created the world's first radio quiz show. This was broadcast in Toronto in 1935. He went on to devise and emcee such popular radio and television quiz programs as "Take a Chance" and "Fun Parade." He retired to Victoria in 1968 and published *The Greatest Quiz Book Ever*. What was his name?
2. Immensely popular was "Treasure _____," which was conceived by Jack Murray and produced for Wrigley's Gum. Originated by CFRB in Toronto in 1937, it was carried across the country by seven stations, later by the CBC. Shows were produced in Vancouver, Winnipeg, and Toronto, with a separate French production out of Montreal. It attracted 100,000 letters a week and lasted into the 1950s.
3. What was the name of the radio quiz program that originated in Toronto, that was heard from 1945 to 1956, and that opened with Cy Mack or Stan Francis shouting: "Gold, silver, dollars . . . gold, silver, dollars . . . gold, silver, dollars . . . money, money, money!"
4. Heard on national radio from 1950 to 1969 was "Now I Ask You," which began with the moderator saying, in his thick Scots accent: "Well, gentlemen, now I ask you. . . ." Listeners sent in questions which were checked by the quiz master and then identified and discussed by regular panelists. J.B. McGeachy, the moderator, had a nickname, which was _____. The quiz master was poet and writer _____ Hambleton. Three of the regular panelists were _____ Allen, _____ Bannerman, and _____ Callaghan.
5. Although more a discussion program than a quiz show, this fondly remembered radio (1952-62) and television (1953-63) program asked such panelists as Irving Layton and Dr. W.E. Blatz to guess the authors of provocative quotations submitted by listeners and then to discuss them. The program was called _____, and its growly voiced moderator was _____. All opinions were "spontaneous and _____."

126. Saintly Men and Women

Roman Catholics are aware, especially in Quebec, of those men and women who were particularly pious and made contributions to the spiritual needs of their contemporaries. Some have been beatified and even sainted; all inspire devotion. Match up the saintly person with his or her accomplishments.

1. Brother André was . . .

2. Marguerite Bourgeoys is . . .

3. Jean de Brébeuf suffered . . .

4. Isaac Jogues escaped . . .

5. Gabriel Lalemant had . . .

6. Kateri Tekakwitha, known . . .

7. Marguerite d'Youville was . . .

A. martyrdom with Brébeuf but was later captured and killed.

B. the ill-fortune to be tortured and killed in 1649.

C. the founder of both a religious order, Congrégation de Notre-Dame de Montréal, 1671, and a school in Montreal; beatified 1950; sanctified 1982.

D. as the Lily of the Mohawks, died at the age of twenty-four.

E. the inspiration behind the building of St. Joseph's Oratory in Montreal.

F. martyrdom at Saint-Ignace; he wrote two accounts of the Huron Missions.

G. the founder of the Grey Nuns and head of the Hôpital-Général, Montreal.

127. Patron Saints

There is a saint for every person, for every occasion, for every employment, for every country of the world. Find out how well you know your saintly lore by answering the following questions which are about saints with some connection with the people of Canada.

1. St. Andrew is the patron saint of _____. His feast day is 30 November.
2. St. _____ is the patron saint of Wales. 1 March is the day reserved for him.
3. St. George is the patron saint of _____. The day of his feast is 23 April.
4. St. _____ is the patron saint of Ireland. 17 March is the day designated for him.
5. St. Denis (or Denys) is the patron saint of _____. He is honored on 9 October.
6. _____, according to the Roman Catholic Church, is the patron saint of Canada. His feast day is 24 _____.
7. In the New Testament the patron saint of Canada is described as "the _____ of one _____ in the _____." In 1487, on his feast day, which coincides with his birthday, John _____ made his historic landfall in Eastern Canada. In the Province of Quebec, the _____ takes special pride in arranging parades and other events to honor the patron saint of Canada.

128. Religious Questions

Religion may be a private matter, yet its expression takes place in the world. Thus it is subject to historical inquiry and questioning. These questions are concerned not so much with religious beliefs as with the expression of the religious spirit in Canada yesterday and today.

1. What is the meaning of the Algonkian word *Manitou*?
2. Founded in 1528, they believe that true Christianity can be practiced only in communal living. Name the sect.
3. With whom are the following lines associated?

   'Twas in the moon of wintertime
   When all the birds had fled,
   That Mighty Gitchi Manitou
   Sent angel choirs instead.

4. In early Canada until 1854, the so-called Clergy Reserves caused endless problems. What were Clergy Reserves and why did all problems cease in 1854?
5. A notorious imposter was Maria Monk. Who was she and what did she do?
6. A native of Newfoundland, Richard Brothers (1757-1824) called himself "Nephew of the Almighty" and believed the British people to be descendants of the Ten Lost Tribes. What group today holds essentially the same beliefs?
7. James Evans was superintendent of Wesleyan missions in the Northwest. At Norway House in 1841, he made "a gift to a nation of a written tongue." Which "nation" received this gift, and what evidence exists that it is still in use?
8. What was the name of the Englishman who adapted Psalm 121 into the

125

hymn "Unto the Hills," after viewing the Rocky Mountains in the late 1870s?

9. This sect was organized by Menno Simmons after the bloody suppression of Anabaptists who tried to create a "New Jerusalem" in Münster, Germany. Persecuted in Europe and Russia, thousands fled to the Canadian Prairies after 1873. They believe in non-resistance and reject infant baptism and civil magistracy. Who are they?

10. Who wanted to re-establish the Pope in the Canadian West, to rename the North Star "Henrietta," and to inform everyone that he believed himself to be "the prophet of the New World"?

11. A pacifist Russian sect dating from the mid-eighteenth century, they are agrarian and hold property in common. One militant group was helped by Leo Tolstoy to emigrate to Canada in 1898-99. They adopted the name — "spirit wrestlers" — assigned by their opponents. Who are they?

12. In 1901, Richard Maurice Bucke published a study of the religious experience that elicited admiration from William James and has been a steady seller ever since. It added a new phrase to the language. What is the title of this book?

13. In 1925, all the Methodists, virtually all the Congregationalists, and two-thirds of the Presbyterians of Canada joined a newly created body, which is now the country's largest Protestant denomination. What is its name?

14. Who wrote these lines about the source of an early missionary's spiritual strength?

    . . . not in these the source —
    But in the sound of invisible trumpets blowing
    Around two slabs of board, right-angled, hammered
    By Roman nails and hung on a Jewish hill.

15. Charlotte Whitton, when mayor of Ottawa, told an interviewer in 1951: "My mother's a Catholic. My father was an Orangeman. Where does that leave me? Right in the _____ Church." Fill in the blank.

16. Our Lady of Victory is the name of a church in Inuvik, N.W.T. It has an unusual distinction. It is shaped like an _____, being built of blocks of wood painted white which are surmounted by a bronze dome.

17. The Anglican Church of Canada was so named in 1955. What was it called before?

18. "Today, rather than pretend to an atheism that can no more be proved than can the existence of God, I prefer to think that _____ is the only *modest* faith." So wrote Vilhjalmur Stefansson, the Arctic explorer, in his autobiographical *Discovery*. Fill in the blank.

19. In 1965, a Pierre Berton book launched a national debate on the relevance of the church to modern Canadian society. What was this book called?

20. What Ukrainian-Canadian artist painted an awe-inspiring canvas called *Northern Nativity* which depicts the infant Jesus in Mary's arms in an igloo?

21. The tallest church in the country is in Montreal. What is its name?

22. In the Census of 1971, three out of four persons in Canada reported they belonged to one of the three largest denominations. Name the denominations.

23. Where is "God's Country"?

RESOURCES

129. Natural Resources

The true wealth of Canada will be found in the minds and wills of
Canadians. Buried in the ground lies the nation's mineral wealth. The
extraction, refinement, and fabrication of such wealth creates jobs.
Geologists divide mineral products into four groups — the metallics, the
non-metallics, the fuels, and the structural materials. Listed below (left) are
these four categories and (right) ten leading mineral products. Arrange the
mineral products by group, then arrange them alphabetically within each
group.

Metallics

1.

2.

3.

4.

Non-Metallics

5.

6.

Fuels

7.

8.

Structural Materials

9.

10.

A. Asbestos.

B. Cement.

C. Copper.

D. Crude Oil.

E. Iron Ore.

F. Natural Gas.

G. Nickel.

H. Potash.

I. Sand and Gravel.

J. Zinc.

130. Mineral Production

Canada produces about sixty different minerals. Over eighty percent of the mineral production is exported, with the biggest market being the United States, followed by Japan, the European Economic Community, and the United Kingdom. In this quiz, some major and minor minerals are listed by province or territory of production. Identify the minerals in question. After doing that, identify four minerals that Canada imports.

1. Alberta: _ _ _ _ OLEUM.   _ _ _ PHUR.
2. British Columbia: CO _ _ ER.   _ INC.
3. Manitoba: _ _ CK _ _.   _ _ PP _ _.
4. New Brunswick: Z _ _ C.   _ _ AD.
5. Newfoundland: _ _ ON _ R _.   _ _ _ ORSPAR.
6. Nova Scotia: _ _ AL.   GY _ _ _ M.
7. Ontario: NI _ _ EL. QU _ _ _ Z.   SU _ _ _ UR.
8. Prince Edward Island: _ AND & G _ _ _ EL.
9. Quebec: COP _ _ _.   _ _ BEST _ _.
10. Saskatchewan: POT _ _ _.   _ _ ANI _ _.
11. Northwest Territories: ZI _ _.   _ _ LVER.
12. Yukon Territory: L _ _ D.   ASB _ _ _ _ _.
13. Canada imports the following minerals:
    MAN _ _ _ ESE.   _ _ ROMI _ _.   _ _ UXIT _.   _ I _.

---

131. Black Gold

"Black gold" is a nickname for oil, much favored by old-time prospectors but not much heard these days. This quiz is concerned with some highlights in the development of Canada's oil industry.

1. The world's first commercial oil well that was drilled rather than dug was developed in 1947 at:

   A. Leduc, near Edmonton, Alta.
   B. Oil Springs, near Sarnia, Ont.
   C. Happy Valley, near Calgary, Alta.

2. What is now the country's largest oil company was founded by a group of Toronto businessmen with the help of Standard Oil of New Jersey in 1880. What is the company called?

3. The date February 1947 is an important one in the resource history of Canada, especially so in the West. What was discovered, and where?

4. In 1971, the Canadian government declared an "economic zone" off the country's shores. How many kilometres does this zone extend from land? As well as declaring Canada's sovereignty over Arctic and other waters, it protects Canadian fishing and off-shore _____.

5. A Crown corporation was formed and located in Calgary in 1975 to develop petroleum and oversee Canada's oil needs. What is it called?

6. The bitumen-rich Athabasca Tar Sands are located in the northeast section of which province?

7. Canada's deposits of Arctic gas and oil are principally located in the Mackenzie Delta and in Prudhoe Bay and the Beaufort Sea. Is the Mackenzie Delta part of the Yukon Territory or the Northwest Territories?

8. Which province will benefit more than any other province from the development of the Hibernia deposits?

9. In 1977, Chief Justice Thomas Berger tabled his report on the desirability of constructing the Mackenzie Valley Pipeline to bring Arctic gas and oil to markets in the south. He recommended:

A. Immediate construction of the pipeline.
B. A ten-year moratorium on pipeline construction.
C. Use of existing tankers to future pipelines.
D. Wholesale relocation of the native population.

132. Time on Your Hands

"Myself and time against any two men," boasted Sir John A. Macdonald. How much time will it take you to answer these seven questions, all based on the lore and learning connected with the reckoning of time in Canada?

1. Sir Sandford Fleming was a Canadian engineer who, in 1879, proposed an international system for determining local time. It was adopted five years later. What is it called?

2. If a mnemonic is something that jogs the memory, what does the mnemonic "Spring forward, fall back" remind one to do?

3. A line of graffiti runs: "The world will come to an end at 12:00 midnight — 12:30 in Newfoundland." What truth does it contain?

4. Canada is divided into seven time zones, the globe into twenty-four. By convention, time is reckoned or measured from the Observatory at Greenwich, England. If Greenwich Mean Time is 12:00, what time is it in the seven time zones of Canada?
   A. Newfoundland.   i. 4:00.
   B. Atlantic.   ii. 3:00.
   C. Eastern.   iii. 5:00.
   D. Central.   iv. 8:30.
   E. Mountain.   v. 7:00.
   F. Pacific.   vi. 8:00.
   G. Yukon.   vii. 6:00.

5. If it is 11:00 A.M. in Ottawa, what time is it in the following locales?
   A. Saint John, N.B.   D. Quebec.
   B. Winnipeg.   E. Dawson City, Y.T.
   C. Barkerville, B.C.   F. Newfoundland.

6. The Twenty-four Hour Clock is being increasingly used in hospitals, in

130

travel, etc. It is not as confusing as it looks. Convert these 24-hour figures to 12-hour figures or *vice versa*.

A. 3:17 A.M.   D. 1:24 P.M.
B. 12:00 noon.   E. 12:00 midnight.
C. 08:18.   F. 13:45.

---

133. Discoveries and Inventions

This quiz pays tribute to those Canadian scientists and researchers who have made discoveries or inventions that have enriched human life. Of the hundreds of names and devices that could be mentioned, here are twenty-five — some amazing, some amusing — but all of them Canadian "firsts." Match the scientist or researcher with the discovery or invention.

1. F.W. (Casey) Baldwin.
2. Frederick G. Banting.
3. Alexander Graham Bell.
4. J. Armand Bombardier.
5. Norman Breakey.
6. Thomas Carroll.
7. Frederick Creed.
8. G. E. Desbarats.
9. Robert Foulis.
10. W.R. Fraks.
11. Abraham Gesner.
12. James Guillet.
13. James Hillier.
14. Arthur Irwin.
15. Harold Johns.
16. Joseph MacInnis.
17. John McLennan.
18. Steve Pasjack.
19. Tommy Ryan.
20. Charles E. Saunders.
21. Arthur Sicard.
22. William Stephenson.
23. W.R. Turnbull.
24. James Miller Williams.
25. Thomas L. Willson.
26. J. Tuzo Wilson.

A. Theory of plate tectonics.
B. Calcium carbide production.
C. First commercially successful oil well.
D. Variable-pitch propellor.
E. First successful radio-transmitted newspaper photograph.
F. First snowblower.
G. Marquis wheat grown.
H. Five-pin bowling devised.
I. Tuck-away beer-carton handle.
J. Extraction of helium.
K. Sub-igloo and Sub-mersible.
L. Cobalt "bomb" research.
M. Padded baseball glove devised.
N. Electron microscope built.
O. Degradable plastic research.
P. Kerosene production.
Q. Flying suit perfected.
R. First steam foghorn.
S. Earliest half-tone reproduction.
T. Creed Telegraph System devised.
U. Self-propelled combine harvester.
V. Paint roller devised.
W. First snowmobile.
X. Telephone invented.
Y. Isolation of insulin.
Z. First to fly in a plane.

---

134. Famous Physicians

"The practice of medicine is an art, based on science," wrote Sir William Osler. Canada has had any number of these artists or scientists —

distinguished historical figures, practicing physicians and surgeons, medical researchers, etc. Two hundred could be listed, and then some. Instead, here is a quiz based on twenty well-known healers. Match up their names and dates with their principal contributions, bearing in mind that many were or are multi-talented and have made substantial contributions in more than a single field.

1. Edward A. Archibald (1872-1959).

2. Sir Frederick C. Banting (1891-1941).

3. Murray Barr (born 1908).

4. Wilfred A. Bigelow (1879-1966).

5. Alan Brown (1887-1960).

6. James B. Collip (1892-1965).

7. Edward A. Gallie (1882-1959).

8. Gustave Gingras (born 1918).

9. Sir Wilfred Grenfell (1865-1940).

10. Abraham Groves (1847-1935).

11. Clarence M. Hincks (1885-1964).

12. Mahlon W. Locke (1881-1942).

13. Cluny MacPherson (1879-1966).

14. Henry Morgentaler (born 1922).

15. Gordon Murray (1896-1976).

16. Sir William Osler (1849-1919).

17. Wilder Penfield (1891-1976).

A. Earliest of French surgeons in Quebec; authority on epidemics and natural history.

B. Performed the world's first elective appendectomy; employed aseptic and new surgical techniques.

C. A world authority on techniques for the rehabilitation of the handicapped.

D. Leading neurosurgeon who greatly enlarged the field of study and treatment of the brain.

E. Specialist in manipulative surgery and orthopedics; fabled as a healer of arthritis.

F. Discoverer of the sex chromatin, a female characteristic, now named the "Barr body."

G. Developed the concept of the General Adaptation Syndrome, commonly called "stress concept."

H. Specialist in surgery and tendon fixation, including the "Gallie living suture."

I. Pioneer in the use of blood transfusion and techniques of X-ray examination.

J. Founded the International Grenfell Association to provide care for people of Labrador and Newfoundland.

K. Pioneer in therapeutic abortion techniques and in the establishment of clinics.

L. Called "the most influential physician since Hippocrates"; outstanding clinician, teacher, and writer.

M. Widely heeded pediatrician and teacher; noted for his organizational ability and withering wit.

N. A pioneer in thoracic surgery; leading teacher of scientific surgical techniques.

O. Concerned with public health; he developed the first effective gas mask.

P. Isolated insulin pure enough for human use; inspired subsequent research and influenced course of medical education.

Q. Authority on mental problems; established first mental-health clinic in Canada.

18. Michel Sarrazin (1659-1734).	**R.** Developed the first successful artificial kidney in North America; pioneered in cardiac surgery.
19. Hans Selye (1907-1982).	**S.** Respected pediatrician and nutritionist; with Drs. Alan Brown and T.G.H. Drake developed the precooked baby's cereal, Pablum.
20. Frederick Tisdall (1893-1949).	**T.** Worked on purification of insulin; isolated parathormone, active principle of thyroid gland; worked on hormones.

135. Space Age

There is a message from Canada on the surface of the moon. It is one of seventy-three succinct statements made by world leaders which were miniaturized and reproduced on a disc the size of a fifty-cent piece. It was taken to the moon aboard the Apollo flight and deposited on the lunar surface by Neil Armstrong, 20 July 1969. The message, drafted by Prime Minister Trudeau, is bilingual and runs: "Man has reached out and touched the tranquil moon. Puisse ce haut fait permettre à l'homme de redécouvrir la terre et d'y trouver la paix. [May that high accomplishment allow man to rediscover the earth and there find peace.]" Here are questions on Canadian contributions to astronomy, atomic energy, communications technology, and space-age hardware.

1. It was a great spectacle. The evening of 9 Feb. 1913, the night sky across Saskatchewan, Manitoba, and Ontario was illuminated by a stream of meteorites that was visible for over three minutes. "It moved forward in a perfectly horizontal path, with peculiar majestic, dignified deliberation," wrote C.A. Chant, Professor of Astronomy, University of Toronto, who studied the phenomenon in detail. The spectacle is generally called Chant's _____.

2. The site of Canada's first nuclear reactor is at Chalk _____. In 1952, the AECL was formed to co-ordinate atomic research. AECL stands for _____. The world's largest operating nuclear power-generating station is located at _____, Ont. Canada's reactor design, which uses natural rather than enriched _____, is considered the safest in the world. It is called the _____ reactor.

3. Canada contributed the first satellite designed and built by a nation other than the United States and the Soviet Union. This was the _____ satellite, which was launched on 29 Sept. 1962. Canada also contributed the world's first geostationary communications satellite. This was called _____, and it was launched on 9 Nov. 1972. The Crown corporation concerned with telecommunication services via satellites is called _____ Canada.

4. What was Operation Morning Light? (Clue No. 1: It commenced, in effect, on 24 Jan. 1978. Clue No. 2: It concerned the Northwest Territories and, by implication, the rest of the world.)

5. The United States has its so-called Silicon Valley, outside Los Angeles, where microcircuits are designed and manufactured. Canada has its equivalent just southwest of Ottawa, and it is called _____.

6. In August 1978, the Communications Research Centre of the Department of Communications unveiled its two-way communication system that links television sets to computers and memory banks. This videotex system is called _____.

7. The Space Shuttle *Columbia* went into orbit on 22 March 1982. In its payload bay was an innovative remote manipulator arm 15 metres (50 feet) long, capable of articulation at three joints. The arm, designed and built by the National _____ and Spar _____ of Toronto, is known as the "Canad_____."

SPORTS

136. Outsiders

Some outsiders have tried to crash the team rosters. Spot the sportsman whose sport is not the same as that of the other two, in each of the threesomes that follow. Know your sport?

1. Sid Abel. George Armstrong. George Athans.
2. Frenchie Belanger. Marilyn Bell. Tommy Burns.
3. George Chuvalo. Johnny Coulson. Bill Crothers.
4. Ken Doraty. Yvon Durelle. Bill Durnan.
5. Jim Elder. Ron Ellis. Phil Esposito.
6. Bernie Faloney. Jim Foley. Lou Fontinato.
7. Charles Graham. Johnny Greco. Charlie Gorman.
8. Ned Hanlan. Bill Hayward. George Hungerford.
9. Punch Imlach. Dick Irvin Sr. Cathy Lee Irwin.
10. Harry Jerome. Ching Johnson. Aurel Joliat.
11. Bruce Kidd. Dan Kulai. Doug Kyle.
12. Sam Langford. Stan Leonard. George S. Lyon.
13. Nancy McCredie. Earl McCready. Jackie MacDonald.
14. Eric Nesterenko. Lynn Nightingale. Frank Nighbor.
15. Zeke O'Connor. Tip O'Neill. Steve Oneschuk.
16. J. Percy Page. Bob Phibbs. Jack Purcell.
17. Bruce Rogers. Ernestine Russell. Gus Ryder.
18. Bill Sherring. Sandy Somerville. Marilyn Stewart Streit.
19. Linda Thom. Arthur Tomsett. Ron Turcotte.
20. Eileen Underhill. John Underhill. Faye Urban.
21. Michel Vaillancourt. Donna Valaitis. Debbie Van Kiekebelt.
22. Bill Wagner. Ken Watson. George Woolf.
23. Wayne Yetman. Joe Young. Jane Youngberg.

137. Addagrams

An addagram is a puzzle in which the letters of the mystery word are suppressed and must be supplied using the clues provided. The object is to fill in the blank spaces with the letters of the mystery word. The mystery words are those of sports that appeal to single competitors (A-H) as well as team sports and games (I-U).

A.

1	2	3	4	5	6	7	8	9	10

1, 2, 3 — where one works out.
4, 5, 6, 7 — mean, without the last y.
7, 8, 9, 10 — twitchings.

B.

1	2	3	4	5	6	7	8

1, 3, 7, 8 — what opera stars do.
2, 6, 7, 8 — what a bird has.
4, 5 — Roman two thousand.

C.

1	2	3	4	5	6	7

1, 2, 5 — second person singular of *to be*.
3, 4, 5, 6 — U.S. popular singer.
7 — second-last letter.

D.

1	2	3	4	5	6	7	8	9	10	11	12	13

1, 2, 6 — what water is.
3 — first person singular.
4, 8, 9, 10 — a present.
5, 11, 12, 13 — doors move on (sans e).
7, 8, 9, 10 — to raise aloft.

E.

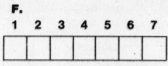

1 2 3 4 5 6 7 8

1, 2, 3 — to disfigure.

4, 5 — common preposition.

6, 7, 5 — opposite of cold.

4, 5, 7, 8 — name of Egyptian god.

F.

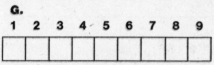

1 2 3 4 5 6 7

1, 3, 4 — past tense of *to sit*.

2, 5, 6, 7 — a male monarch.

G.

1 2 3 4 5 6 7 8 9

1, 3, 4, 5 — a cardinal direction.

2, 3, 4, 5 — to relax.

4, 6, 7, 8, 9 — as in shot.

H.

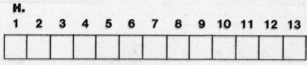

1 2 3 4 5 6 7 8 9 10 11 12 13

1, 3, 4, 5 — as in thumb.

2, 6, 7 — past tense of *to run*.

8 — Roman five hundred.

9, 11, 13 — as in . . . up; tired of.

10, 12 — two-thirds of *ill*.

I.

1 2 3 4 5 6 7 8 9

1, 2, 3 — opposite of good.

4, 5, 6, 7 — a kind of candy.

5, 6 — a common preposition.

7, 8, 9 — two thousand pounds.

J.

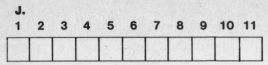

1, 6, 7 — what one sleeps in.
2, 7, 8 — peculiar.
3, 9, 11 — large.
4, 5, 6, 7 — sleigh.
9, 10 — common preposition.

K.

1	2	3	4	5	6

1, 2, 3, 4 — to pawn.
4, 5, 6 — lock and . . . .

L.

1	2	3	4	5	6	7	8	9	10

1, 5, 6 — to wager.
2, 3, 4 — to question.
7, 8, 9, 10 — where Cinderella went.

M.

1, 2, 3 — something made of tin.
3, 4 — opposite of yes.
2, 5, 6, 4 — four of five vowels.
7, 8 — two-thirds of nag.

N.

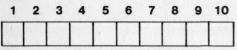

1, 7, 9 — a period of time.
2, 3, 4, 5, 6 — a search.
8, 10 — a common preposition.

O.

1, 6, 7, 8 — to trip.
1, 3, 5 — a watch used to have one.
4, 2 — a common preposition.

P.

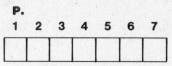

1, 4, 5, 6, 7 — to hold on to.
2, 3 — old word for ancient.

Q.

1, 2 — a university degree.
2, 3 — a subordinate conjunction.
3, 4, 6 — a body of water.
5, 6 — an oil company.
6, 7, 8 — totality.

R.

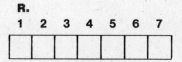

1, 2 — the original "10."
2, 3, 4 — a night bird.
5, 6 — a common preposition.
7, 2, 5, 6, 7 — present progressive of *to go*.

S.

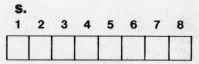

1, 2, 3 — French for *lake*.
4, 5, 6, 8 — a red flower.
7, 8, 2 — a body of water.

T.

1	2	3	4	5	6

1, 2, 3 — metric base number.

5, 6 — third person singular of *to be*.

4, 2, 1 — fish sometimes caught in.

U.

1	2	3	4	5

1, 2, 3 — a mat.

4, 5 — please stand . . . .

---

138. Boxing Ring

This boxing ring is really a complicated puzzle that should be a knock-out for the boxing fan. Around the edge of the square ring appear the last names of outstanding boxers from the past and present. The names may read: from left to right, from right to left; from top to bottom, from bottom to top; with some letters used once, with other letters used twice. In the ring, as if sparring, are the names — first names this time — of two leading fighters. The boxers' names are scrambled — it has been a rough fight — but the names around the ring are not scrambled.

```
E  B  U  R  N  S  A  N  D
L                       U
A                       L
N     V  O  N  Y        O
G                       L
E        A  L  G  E     A
R                       V
N                       U
I  N  R  A  L  C  M  C  H
```

140

139. Gridiron Maze

Here is an *amazing* array of footballers' names. Those bold enough to tackle this gridiron maze will find one dozen names of football personalities of the past and present. Look for the last names — from left to right, from top to bottom. Look below for clues in the form of first names plus identifying details. Set a time limit — a quarter-hour?

1. Jim _____, EFC all-star.
2. Leo _____, Argos coach.
3. John _____, manager-player-coach.
4. Lefty _____, WFC all-star.
5. John _____, "The Bull."
6. Steve _____, EFC all-star.
7. Steve _____, now M.P.
8. Jackie _____, B.C. Lions.
9. Harvey _____, all-rounder.
10. Ralph _____, Ti-Cats.
11. Annis _____, Canucks.
12. John _____, defensive backfielder.

```
O   N   E   T   R   A   F   O   R   D   A   R
N   H   E   N   D   R   I   C   K   S   O   N
E   I   L   L   O   P   A   P   R   A   S   A
S   F   E   R   R   A   R   O   R   Z   R   N
C   A   R   K   H   P   U   L   F   O   R   D
H   W   Y   D   A   R   E   N   Y   K   Q   R
U   C   A   H   I   O   S   K   I   W   Y   E
K   A   S   V   W   S   T   U   K   U   S   O
R   H   P   A   R   K   E   R   F   G   U   T
N   I   S   A   Z   I   O   A   E   N   Y   T
O   L   D   J   M   E   T   R   A   S   C   I
U   L   F   O   R   U   K   U   A   R   O   M
```

140. Olympic Individualists

The Olympic Games are the most demanding athletic competition in the world. A number of Canada's Olympic Gold Medallists have had to demonstrate not only extraordinary ability but also incredible determination, as witnessed by the ordeals of the following (selected for special mention by Frank Cosentino and Glynn Leyshon in *Olympic Gold: Canada's Winners in the Summer Games* [1975]).

1. He was Canada's first individual Gold Medallist. He had to quit his job as a Montreal police constable to compete in the St. Louis games of 1904, where he threw a weight 34'4" and won the 56-pound weight throw. He was the only non-American to win a gold medal in track and field. Known as "Mr. Hammer," his real name was . . .

   A. Francis Amyot.

2. He won his Gold in that most Greek of competitions, the Marathon, in Athens in 1906. The 5'6" runner had only $75 to pay his expenses from Hamilton, Ont., so he or a friend bet all of it on a horse that paid six-to-one, and won! After his victory the mayor of Hamilton handed him a purse of $5,000. His name was . . .

   B. Percy Williams.

3. He was only 19 years old and 126 pounds when he competed at Amsterdam in 1928. As a child in Vancouver, he had suffered rheumatic fever, yet he persisted and evolved a sprint style which permitted him to shift speeds. He worked his way from Vancouver to Toronto for the Olympic trials by serving as a waiter in the train dining car. He took two Golds — 100 metres and 200 metres. Two years later he pulled a thigh muscle and "The World's Fastest Human" never regained his former speed.

   C. Ethel Catherwood.

4. She competed in the 1928 Amsterdam games the first year that track-and-field events were opened to women competitors. Against Dutch and U.S. favorites, she took the Gold Medal in High Jump. Although she was only 5'2" in height, she sailed over the bar officially measured at 5'2 3/5" (record books specify 5'3"). She won the beauty prize awarded by a correspondent of the *New York Times*. She was called "The Saskatoon Lily," and her return to that city occasioned the largest reception in its history.

   D. Bill Sherring.

5. He may have been the Dominion's senior canoeist on six occasions, but as coach, manager, and member of the Canadian team

   E. Étienne Desmarteau.

for the 1936 Berlin Olympics, the Ottawa native had to raise the money himself. Once there he entered the 1,000-metre paddling event. Despite the fact that the Canadian training canoe was 45 pounds lighter than the European racing canoe, he won the event and Canada's only Gold in 1936 — Canadian singles canoeing.

---

141. Confusables

How much of a sports-follower are you? Can you distinguish the sports notables who are confusables? Answer the following questions to find out how knowledgeable you are about sports across the board.

1. Dick Adams plays football. Henry Adams curls. Jack Adams plays hockey. In what sport did Bob Adams compete?
2. Here are five personalities who answer to the same last name. What is it? Don is a curler and golfer; Gabby is a baseball player; George is a soccer player; Les is in archery; and Verne is a skier.
3. Ethel Babbitt, and her two children John and Isobel, all excel in _____.
4. Bobby and his brother David _____ were both involved in hockey; the same is true of the Bentley brothers, _____ and _____.
5. George, Bill, Frank, and Bob _____ are all notable, Ottawa-born hockey players.
6. Lou Bruce competed in football, whereas Bruce Kidd competed in _____.
7. Both Burkas are superb skaters, with _____ being the figure skater and _____ the speed skater.
8. Does Bobby Clarke play football and Bill Clarke hockey, or *vice versa*?
9. Yvan Cornouyer and Alex Delveicchio are fine hockey players but their names are hard to spell. Are they correctly spelled here?
10. Here are three odd-sounding names: Eon, Ion, and Keon. They belong to Suzanne Eon, Mickey Ion, and Dave Keon. In no special order they are top achievers in hockey, hockey and lacrosse, and synchronized swimming. Which does what?
11. John _____ is a hockey player. _____ Jenkins is a baseball player. One thing they have in common is a name, John's second and Jenkins's first. What is it?
12. There are six, sports-minded Jacksons (in addition to the smoker Peter Jackson). Match them up with their sports.
    A. Busher.   i. Football.
    B. Don.   ii. Hockey.
    C. Donald.   iii. Archery.
    D. Robbie.   iv. Figure skating.
    E. Roger.   v. Golf.
    F. Russ.   vi. Rowing.
13. The bandleader, Guy Lombardo, was a Gold Cup winner in his chosen field. What was it?
14. The football player was Neil Lumsden, the hockey player was Chuck

Lumsden, and the swimmer is Cliff Lumsdon. Or is it the other way round? (Bonus question: Which one has the athletic daughter named Kim?)

15. Frank and Pete are brothers so they have the same last name. They also have the same calling — hockey. What is their last name?

16. Name Denis Potvin's hockey-playing brother.

17. Barbara Ann Scott may be a champion figure skater, but she is not the only sports-minded Scott. There is also Alex Scott (curling) and _____ Scott (football).

18. There are two Stewarts. One was born in Toronto and played football. The other was born in Calgary and played hockey. What are their first names?

19. Allyn, June, Masao, Philip, Ray, and Tina Takahashi excel at which sport?

20. Ken Watson was a curler, whereas Whipper Billy Watson was a _____.

142. Some New Trophies

Sports federations and athletic associations frequently — usually annually — honor sports figures by presenting them with trophies, medals, and awards. Perhaps some new trophies are needed to honor sports excellence. The new trophies would retrospectively honor men and women who were outstanding in varied fields. Here are some imaginary awards. Answer the questions based on familiar names and familiar sports but fictitious trophies!

1. For what sport would you receive the George Beers Trophy? What did he do in that discipline?

2. We need the Cheevers Cup to honor achievement in which field?

3. The Chuvalo Medal would go to an outstanding _____. Give Chuvalo's first name.

4. The Christilot Cup or the Elder Medal should be established by which association? Whom would they honor?

5. The Garapick Cup goes to _____. What is Garapick's first name?

6. Why would it be appropriate to design a round, white Knudson Trophy?

7. The Kreiner Cup could honor achievement in _____. It should have two handles, of course, one for _____ and the other for _____.

8. A top _____ should receive the Magnussen Medal. What is Magnussen's first name?

9. Why would an award designed with a bullseye be appropriate for the Susan Nattrass Award?

10. If they establish a medal for _____ it should bear the name of Percy Page.

11. Some day there may well be the Orr Award for outstanding achievement in _____.

12. The Lloyd Percival Trophy could go for physical fitness but also for performance in _____.

13. To be truly symbolic, the Gus Ryder Medal should be pinned onto what item of sports apparel? Why?

14. People would burn rubber to receive the Villeneuve Cup. Why?

143. Confusion at the NHL

Because of confusion or computer error in its Montreal headquarters, the National Hockey League issued a list of its twenty professional clubs with the club names in garbled form. If you are a hockey fan — and hockey is the most popular professional sport in the country — you should, without any difficulty at all, be able to right the wrongs committed below.

1. Boston Canucks.
2. Buffalo Blues.
3. Calgary Whalers.
4. Chicago Kings.
5. Colorado Jets.
6. Detroit Flyers.
7. Edmonton Rangers.
8. Hartford Bruins.
9. Los Angeles Nordiques.
10. Minnesota Maple Leafs.
11. Montreal Rockies.
12. New York Canadiens.
13. New York Capitals.
14. Philadelphia Flames.
15. Quebec Red Wings.
16. St. Louis Oilers.
17. Toronto Islanders.
18. Vancouver North Stars.
19. Washington Sabres.
20. Winnipeg Black Hawks.

144. Sweater Numbers

In hockey there is a mystique about the numbers players wear on their sweaters. In the numerology of hockey, Number 9 is the coveted and magical number. Whoever wears it is a "hockey great." Here is some lore about the mystique of sweater numbers.

1. "Number 4, Bobby Orr." It even rhymes. The number was also worn by a player (now coach) of the Montreal Canadiens. Name him.
2. He led the Leafs to their first Stanley Cup, and he alone wore Number 7. Name him.
3. The mystique of Number 9 is such that one should be able to identify the players who donned this sweater by their initials alone: GH, BH, TK, MR. Name these leading players.
4. Eleven is made up of two one's. His nickname is made up of the same sound repeated. Who is he?
5. Number 13 may be unlucky for some, but not for him, although when he struck an official and was suspended it triggered a Montreal Forum riot. Who is he?
6. A Czech and a Swede both wore Number 21. Name them.
7. Both Darryl and Frank donned Number 27. Give their last names.
8. If 9 is a magical number, what about Number 99 — multi-magic? Name the player who currently wears this number sweater.

145. Sports Nicknames

Sports personalities seem to sport more nicknames and monickers than members of any other group. Here, from the Honour Roll of Members admitted to Canada's Sports Hall of Fame between 1969 and 1981, are the officially recognized nicknames. Match the monicker with the sports personality.

1.	Cap.	A.	Hawley Welch (football).
2.	Cyclone.	B.	Hector Blake (hockey).
3.	Dit.	C.	Frank R. Leadley (football).
4.	Dynamite.	D.	Levi Rodgers (rowing).
5.	Huck.	E.	Edouard Lalonde (hockey).
6.	Kid.	F.	Aubrey Clapper (hockey).
7.	Newsy.	G.	Richard Howard (boxing).
8.	Pep.	H.	Leonard Kelly (hockey).
9.	Red.	I.	A.H. Fear (football).
10.	Shotty.	J.	Fred Taylor (hockey).
11.	Silver.	K.	Eddie James (football).
12.	Toe.	L.	S.P. Quilty (football).

STAGE

146. Miscasting

When the computer at the central casting agency was required to supply lists of threesomes, it was poorly programmed, so it printed lists of twosomes plus one. Instead of three ballet dancers, or three popular singers, it supplied two ballet dancers and a popular singer, or two popular singers and a ballet dancer. This created havoc and led to miscasting. Spot the miscast individual in each line.

1. Erik Bruhn. Evelyn Hart. Harry Somers.
2. Dinah Christie. Claire Hadded. Tom Kneebone.
3. Jean Gascon. Anna Russell. Paxton Whitehead.
4. Margaret Mercier. Vincent Warren. Elwy Yost.
5. William Hutt. William Kilbourn. William Needles.
6. Leslie Bell. Elmer Iseler. Mavor Moore.
7. Burton Cummings. Robin Phillips. Neil Young.
8. Alex Barris. David Steinberg. Alan Thicke.
9. Bill Glassco. Tom Hendry. Michael Snow.
10. Budd Knapp. Ruth Springford. Cy Strange.

147. Guide to Plays

There are fourteen stage plays presented here, twelve by Canadian playwrights, two by foreign playwrights who set their dramatic works on Canadian soil. Each play is described as if it were the premiere production, rather in the manner of a listing in *TV Guide*. Identify the plays from their descriptions.

1. In this dark comedy about a homosexual couple, Richard Monette steals the show dressed like Elizabeth Taylor in *Cleopatra.*

2. An Ontario reformatory is the unlikely locale for this comedy-drama, the New York premiere of which resulted in the founding of a society to help former inmates.

3. Mavor Moore plays the part of the mad visionary in this epic play set in the Northwest at a time of troubles.

4. Hate haunts members of an old Toronto family in 1906 — played by Donald and Murray Davis and their sister Barbara Chilcott, with a mixture of melodrama, mystery, and morality.

5. An impatient Eskimo lad, hunting against his father's advice, learns the meaning of obedience and maturity, in this *Bunraku*-like production.

6. In the streets of Vancouver, a prostitute (played by Frances Hyland) is raped and murdered; her father (played by Chief Dan George) grieves.

7. This witty comedy is an intelligent and dramatic disquisition on Canadian philistinism and the U.S. "brain drain."

8. A quick-change artist, Linda Griffiths plays all three parts with aplomb — the enervating girl-wife, the beleaguered husband-statesman, and the ever-inquisitive journalist.

9. In this well-made, three-act comedy, set in England's Tunbridge Wells and the Manitoba towns of Dyer and Prentice, Norah Marsh does her best to contrast civilized and uncouth values.

10. One of life's innocents returns from the war to Montreal to the only home he has known only to discover that his girlfriend has not waited for him.

A. *Creeps* by David Freeman (Tarragon, Toronto, 1971).

B. *The Donnellys* by James Reaney (Tarragon, Toronto, 1975).

C. *The Ecstasy of Rita Joe* by George Ryga (Vancouver Playhouse, 1967).

D. *Fortune My Foe* by Robertson Davies (Kingston International Players, 1949).

E. *Fortune and Men's Eyes* by John Herbert (Actor's Playhouse, N.Y., 1967).

F. *The Glass Cage* by J.B. Priestley (Crest, Toronto, 1957).

G. *Hosanna* by Michel Tremblay (Tarragon, Toronto, 1974).

H. *Inook and the Sun* by Henry Beissel (Stratford Festival, 1973).

I. *The Land of Promise* by W. Somerset Maugham (West End, London, 1914).

J. *Love and Libel* by Robertson Davies (Royal Alexandra, Toronto, 1959).

11. In this epic of southwestern Ontario, a blood feud erupts in an 1880 murder in Biddulph Township, near London.

12. Based on a popular novel is this serio-comic play about the complications that ensue when a false announcement of an engagement appears in a local paper.

13. The washroom of a sheltered workshop is the setting for this bitter comedy about a group of cerebral palsy victims.

14. This satire on Ottawa bureaucracy — an adaptation of Gogol's *The Inspector General* — takes a strange turn when the folk in the northwest Manitoba town in 1873 discover who their visitor is.

K. *Maggie and Pierre* by Linda Griffiths and Paul Thompson (Passe Muraille, 1979).

L. *The Ottawa Man* by Mavor Moore (Crest, Toronto, 1958).

M. *Riel* by John Coulter (New Play Society, Toronto, 1950).

N. *Tit-Coq* by Gratien Gélinas (MN, Montreal, 1948).

---

148. Music and Drama

Here are the titles of an assortment of pageants, plays with music, revues with skits and songs, dramatic musicals, etc. For each title, choose the statement that describes the production in question.

1. *Anne of Green Gables.*
   A. Elmer Harris's play about love, murder, and a deaf girl in P.E.I. was turned into a musical by Mavor Moore and John Fenwick.
   B. Words and music were written by Don Harron, based on the bestselling book about a girl in a foster home.
   C. The first theatrical presentation in North America includes speeches on Champlain's return and even a "Hymn to Neptune."

2. *Billy Bishop Goes to War.*
   A. Cedric Smith adapted Barry Broadfoot's interviews with survivors of the Depression and added plenty of music and song.
   B. This McGill student revue tells how Princess Aurora Borealis of Mukluko found a husband to retain her country's independence.
   C. John Gray was the playwright and actor Eric Peterson holds the stage, singing, miming, even flying solo.

3. *The Dumbells.*
   A. John Gray was the playwright and actor Eric Peterson holds the stage, singing, miming, even flying solo.
   B. Merton and Albert Plunkett kept the vaudeville troupe together with its topical skits about life in the trenches.
   C. Words and music were written by Don Harron, based on the bestselling book about a girl in a foster home.

4. *Johnny Belinda.*
   A. Elmer Harris's play about love, murder, and a deaf girl in P.E.I. was turned into a musical by Mavor Moore and John Fenwick.
   B. Merton and Albert Plunkett kept the vaudeville troupe together with its topical skits about life in the trenches.
   C. Cedric Smith adapted Barry Broadfoot's interviews with survivors of the Depression and added plenty of music and song.

5. **My Fur Lady.**
   A. Words and music were written by Don Harron, based on the bestselling book about a girl in a foster home.
   B. From 1948 to 1971 with a brief revival in 1977, this was an annual revue of topical and satiric songs, dances, skits, mostly on Canadian subjects.
   C. This McGill student revue tells how Princess Aurora Borealis of Mukluko found a husband to retain her country's independence.

6. **Spring Thaw.**
   A. From 1948 to 1971, with a brief revival in 1977, this was an annual revue of topical and satiric songs, dances, skits, mostly on Canadian subjects.
   B. John Gray was the playwright and actor Eric Peterson holds the stage, singing, miming, even flying solo.
   C. Merton and Albert Plunkett kept the vaudeville troup together with its topical skits about life in the trenches.

7. **Ten Lost Years.**
   A. Elmer Harris's play about love, murder, and a deaf girl in P.E.I. was turned into a musical by Mavor Moore and John Fenwick.
   B. Cedric Smith adapted Barry Broadfoot's interviews with survivors of the Depression and added plenty of music and song.
   C. The first theatrical presentation in North America includes speeches on Champlain's return and even a "Hymn to Neptune."

8. **Le Théatre de Neptune.**
   A. John Gray was the playwright and actor Eric Peterson holds the stage, singing, miming, even flying solo.
   B. Words and music were written by Don Harron, based on the bestselling book about a girl in a foster home.
   C. The first theatrical presentation in North America includes speeches on Champlain's return and even a "Hymn to Neptune."

TELEVISION

149. Telecasting

"All television networks should end with the letters BS," claimed Louis Dudek, aphorist and poet. Whether or not this is so, this set of questions is concerned with the evolution of television in Canada.

1. The Canadian Broadcasting Corporation commenced black-and-white telecasting in September 1952. The first French station on the air was CFBT in _____ on 6 Sept. 1952. The first English station on the air was CBLT in _____ two days later.
2. On English-language television, the first face to be seen was that of the weatherman, _____. He wore _____, despite the fact that he did not need them, and had the endearing habit of concluding his weather forecasts by tossing _____. The first voice to be heard on the air belonged to Gil _____. The first program was produced by Norman _____.
3. The so-called second network was born in 1961. This is the privately owned network. What is it called?
4. After fourteen years of television in Canada, a big change took place. What happened in 1966 to alter the picture?
5. All broadcasting in Canada, whether radio or television, public or private, is regulated by a government body. What is the regulatory commission called?
6. What do the initials CATV stand for?
7. In 1982, the regulatory commission finally authorized the introduction of _____ into Canada. It is likely this will change the picture substantially.

150. Entertainers Galore

Here are some multiple-choice questions based on entertainers associated with radio and television. The questions are in rough chronological order.

1. King Ganam played the fiddle on his own country and western show on CBC-TV in the late 1950s. His first name really was:
   A. King.
   B. Clarence.
   C. Ameen.
   D. Joseph.

2. "People Are Funny" and "Let's Make a Deal," both popular American television shows in the 1960s, were hosted by Canadian-born entertainers. In proper order, who are they?
   A. Al Hamel and Monty Hall.
   B. Monty Hall and Al Hamel.
   C. Art Linkletter and Al Hamel.
   D. Al Hamel and Art Linkletter.
   E. Monty Hall and Art Linkletter.
   F. Art Linkletter and Monty Hall.

3. Lorne Green has many accomplishments to his credit, including three of the four ascribed to him below. What is *not* his accomplishment at all?
   A. Green delivered the National News on CBC Radio.
   B. Green founded the Academy of Radio Arts in Toronto.
   C. Green played the Roman emperor in the Stratford Festival's 1955 production of *Julius Caesar.*
   D. Green created the roles of Ben Cartwright on "Bonanza" and Commander Adama on "Battlestar Galactica."

4. Robert Homme is beloved of children for his appearances on the following CBC-TV program:
   A. "Reach for the Top."
   B. "The Friendly Giant."
   C. "The Polka Dot Door."
   D. "Cariboo Country."

5. Sergeant Renfrew of the Mounties and Big Bobby Clovver, the dumb hockey player, are comic creations of writer and performer:
   A. Dave Broadfoot.
   B. Alan Gould.
   C. Mike McManus.
   D. Larry Zolf.

6. Craig Russell may be an impersonator but Rich Little is known as:
   A. A ventriloquist.
   B. A prestidigitator.
   C. An impressionist.
   D. An announcer.

7. David Steinberg, who was born in Winnipeg, got his break in show business when it was learned:
   A. That he was secretly scripting Johnny Carson's opening monologues.
   B. That he was to marry Suzanne Somers.
   C. That his monologue on Moses led to the cancelation of the Smothers Brothers Comedy Hour.
   D. That his impersonations were appreciated by Bob Hope and Gerald Ford.

8. Al Waxman played Larry King on the CBC-TV series "King of Kensington." Who played Cathy King, his wife?
   A. Barbara Hamilton.
   B. Beatrice Lillie.
   C. Fiona Reid.
   D. Margot Kidder.

9. Dave Thomas and Rick Moranis teamed up to create the comedy team known as the McKenzie Brothers to satirize Canadian beer-drinkers who use the all-duty "Eh?" What are the first names of their characters?
   A. Dave and Rick.
   B. Bob and Doug.
   C. Doug and Dick.
   D. Abercrombie and Fitch.

151. Anyone Watching?

Veteran television viewers should have no problem answering the following questions, or filling in the blanks. All deal with popular, or once-popular, Canadian television programs and personalities.

1. The longest-running weekly entertainment show on Canadian television, begun as a summer replacement in 1957, is a panel show hosted and moderated by Fred Davis. Name the show and its three regular panelists.
2. What have the following men in common: Larry Henderson, Earl Cameron, Stanley Burke, Warren Davis, Lloyd Robertson, Peter Kent, and Knowlton Nash?
3. Who are the hosts most closely identified with the following programs?
   A. "Man Alive."
   B. "The Nature of Things."
   C. "What Will They Think of Next."
4. Who plays the part of Nick Adonidas in the comedy-adventure series "The Beachcombers"?
5. What do the letters SCTV stand for?
6. What is a "Raskymentary"?
7. Who says, "Look up, look up, look 'way up . . ." on the CBC-TV program "The Friendly Giant"?
8. "The Adventures of Pierre _____," shown in 1957, was described by one critic as "Canada's answer to Davey Crockett."

9. What weekly series had Gordon Pinsent as a fighting backbencher?

10. What weekly series had John Vernon as a fighting coroner? Who was the real-life model for this series?

11. Who is the beautiful television personality who created a national controversy in 1959 when she said on national television, "Like most Canadians I'm indifferent to the visit of the Queen"?

12. Who is the long-time host of "Canada A.M.," CTV's early-morning talk, weather, and news program?

13. If "The Galloping Gourmet" met "The Pied Piper of Canada," Graham _____ would shake hands with _____ Gimby.

14. What is the single most popular program on Canadian television?

15. It was controversial and more popular with the public than with the CBC hierarchy. It was produced by Patrick Watson and Douglas Leiterman and it starred, in addition to its producers, John Drainie, Laurier LaPierre, Warner Troyer, Larry Zolf, Robert Hoyt, Ken Lefolii, and Dinah Christie. It was seen Sunday evenings from 1964 to 1966. What was it called?

16. Dating from 1961, this long-running, entertaining, and educational quiz show has local, regional, and national competitions. The question setter is Paul Russell and the executive producer is Sandy Stewart. Name both the English and French versions.

TRANSPORTATION

152. The Rails

"The provinces were literally railroaded into Confederation," noted the humorist Eric Nicol. There is no denying the importance of rail transportation in Canadian history or arguing its influence today. Yet when Pierre Berton published *The National Dream*, his book about the building of the CPR, playwright Bernard Slade quipped, "There has to be something wrong with a country whose National Dream is a railroad."

1. What region of the country was served by the old Intercolonial Railway, chartered in 1836? Into which system was it incorporated eighty-seven years later?

2. In 1859, the world's first sleeping car was designed by Thomas Burnley, shop foreman at the Brantford works of the Buffalo and Lake Huron Railway Company. It was designed for the 1860 visit of the Prince of Wales, the future King _____. It influenced George _____ in the design of his well-known _____ car.

3. Where in Western Canada does the following inscription appear and what is the significance of the event it commemorates? "Here on November 7, 1885, a plain iron spike welded East to West."

4. T.J. McBride of Winnipeg invented and patented a new type of passenger car in 1891. It was popular with both tourists and travelers in Western Canada. Why?

5. The year 1919 saw the formation of a Crown corporation that is a major transportation and communication system. What was it called upon its formation?

6. All railway and telephone service was called to a halt for one minute at 6:25 P.M., 4 August 1922. Who had died?

7. What were the "Selkirks"?

8. A notable event was the Royal Visit of King George VI and Queen Elizabeth, who crossed the country by train from 17 May to 15 June 1939. This was

the first visit to Canada of a reigning monarch. In the memories of millions of Canadians who saw Their Majesties, what detail about the train is foremost?

9. In 1960, Canadian National Railways, the publicly owned system, acquired a "new look." What was changed?

10. The *Rapido* is a fast intercity train introduced between which two cities in 1965? How long does the journey take?

11. In 1971, Canadian Pacific Railway, the privately owned system, acquired a new name. What is it? Who was the most famous general manager in the history of the CPR?

12. Passenger train services of the two systems — private and public — were consolidated in the fall of 1976. The combined system operates under what name?

13. The *Railrodder* is a half-hour comedy released by the National Film Board in 1965. No words are spoken by a famous comic from the silent-movie days as he crosses the country from East to West on a railway track scooter. There are many sight gags, however. What is the name of the comedian who "rides the rails"?

153. Ships of Significance

Canada has so much water, both around and within, it is not surprising that Canadian history is replete with ships of note. Here are some vessels that are famous or simply interesting. Match up the ship and important date (on the left) with the notable incident, event, or characteristic (on the right). Happy sailing!

1. *Accommodation,* 31 Oct. 1809.

A. La Salle built this barque above Niagara Falls, and it was the first sailing vessel on Lake Ontario.

2. *Bluenose,* 26 March 1921.

B. The most famous mystery ship of all time, it was found abandoned off the Azores under full sail.

3. *Brendan,* 7 May 1977.

C. This RCMP motor schooner was the first Canadian vessel to traverse the Northwest Passage. It did so both ways, and is now on display in Vancouver.

4. *Discovery,* 24 June 1611.

D. A Japanese vessel with Sikh passengers, it was denied permission to dock at Vancouver and had to return to Hong Kong.

5. *Erebus* and *Terror,* Sept. 1845.

E. The feasibility of tanker transportation through the Arctic was demonstrated by this U.S. vessel which was guided by the Canadian ice-breaker *John A. Macdonald.*

6. *Gjoa,* 1903-6.

F. John Molson built the first steam boat in Canada, and it made its maiden voyage from Montreal to Quebec with ten passengers.

7. *Grande Hermine,* 1535, 1541.

G. The name in Algonkian means "sorcerer," and the steamer vanished for no known reason on Georgian Bay.

8. *Griffon,* 7 Aug. 1679.

H. American authorities sank this rum-runner in the Gulf of Mexico. The loss of the schooner created an international incident.

9. *I'm Alone,* 20 March 1929.

I. The name honors an early Irish saint, and the vessel, a leather coracle, was built to prove the possibility of early North Atlantic migration.

10. *Komagata Maru,* 23 May 1914.

J. One hundred and eighteen died when this cruise ship caught fire in Toronto harbor.

11. *Laser,* 1970.

K. Cartier's flagship made two voyages to the New World. A replica of the vessel is on display in Quebec City.

12. *Manhattan,* 1969-70.

L. This sloop took the Nova Scotian master mariner, Joshua Slocum, a man who could not swim, around the world alone.

13. *Mary Celeste,* 5 Dec. 1872.

M. Henry Hudson was cast adrift from this vessel in James Bay; in 1789 Captain Vancouver piloted a ship by this name.

14. *Nonsuch,* 29 Sept. 1668.

N. Trapped in ice off King William Island, Sir John Franklin later abandoned his two vessels.

15. *Noronic,* 17 Sept. 1949.

O. This is the name of a line of single-handed racing craft, 3.5 metres (11½ feet) long, designed by Bruce Kirby.

16. *Royal William,* 27 April 1831.

P. Roald Amundsen piloted this craft across the Northwest Passage, and it was the first vessel to do so.

17. *St. Roch,* 1940-42.

Q. This ketch proved the feasibility of the fur trade when it wintered on the east coast of James Bay. There is a replica in Winnipeg.

18. *Spray,* 1895-1909.

R. When it arrived at Gravesend, England, this paddle vessel became the first vessel to cross the Atlantic under steam.

19. *Waubuno,* 22 Nov. 1879.

S. This most famous sailing ship of the century never — hardly ever — lost a race. A replica, also the pride of Nova Scotia, was built in 1963.

---

154. Wings over the World

Aviation is contributing as much to the sense of pan-Canadianism as the railway in its day and radio, television, and telecommunications in ours. Canadians have a particularly distinguished and lively flying history, as these questions show.

1. Canada entered the "air age" with a bang when a famous inventor, along with F.W. (Casey) Baldwin, Glenn Curtiss, J.A.D. McCurdy, and Thomas Selfridge, formed the Aerial Experiment Association in 1907. Who was the famous inventor and in what unlikely place was the Association located?

2. The Association tested a number of craft including the three listed here. Match up the craft with the achievement.

A. *Cygnet I.*

i. This was an experimental hydrofoil designed with Baldwin that reached a speed of 113 kilometres (70 miles) per hour on 9 Sept. 1909.

B. *Silver Dart.*

ii. This was a kite of tetrahedral design that raised Selfridge 51 metres (168 feet) for 7 minutes on 6 Dec. 1907.

C. *Hydrodrome-4.*

iii. This was a famous biplane that carried McCurdy nearly half a mile at a height of 9 metres (30 feet) on 23 Feb. 1909.

3. As the result of the Association's experiments, one of the above-mentioned men became in 1908 the first British subject to fly in a heavier-than-air craft. He later sat in the Nova Scotia legislature. What was his name?

4. Such World War I pilots as George (Billy) Barker, George (Buzz) Beurling, William (Billy) Bishop, Clennel (Punch) Dickins, and Wilfrid (Wop) May were known for their ability to down enemy planes. They were called "Fighter _____."

5. Between 1920, with the first commercial flights into the North, and 1939, with the outbreak of World War II, many of these daring pilots flew passengers and freight in and out of the northern bush and barrens. They were called "_____ Pilots."

6. One hundred flying schools were established across the country to train pilots and others from Canada, Australia, New Zealand, and the United Kingdom. The schools functioned from 1939 to 1945 and Franklin Delano Roosevelt called it "the aerodrome of democracy." Its initials are BCATP. What was it called?

7. To supply "speedy and efficient" air transportation across the country, an act was passed on 10 April 1937 incorporating _____.

8. A few months before he was killed in action in 1941, John Gillespie Magree, Jr., an American pilot flying with the Royal Canadian Mounted Police, wrote a sonnet which expressed the thrill and terror of flight. It was adopted by the RCAF. What is the title of this poem, which begins:

> Oh, I have slipped the surly bonds of earth
> And danced the skies on laughter-silvered wings . . .?

9. Despite the war, or perhaps because of it, ten small airlines in the West and North were amalgamated in 1942 into _____, a privately owned national carrier.

10. This international aircraft was built by Canadair. It was designated DC-4M1, it had a pressurized cabin, and it was powered by a Rolls-Royce engine. It was flown by the publicly owned national airline and it was popularly known as the _____.

11. The blackest day in Canadian aviation history was Friday, 20 Feb. 1959. What happened on that day?

12. In 1965, Canada's publicly owned national carrier acquired a new name. _____ is now among the ten largest airlines in the world. It flies a fleet of 120 aircraft nationally and internationally. Its emblem is a red _____. Its headquarters is in _____.

WOMEN

155. Remarkable Women

A great many women of courage and conviction, talent and ability, have contributed to the early history of Canada. The questions here turn on knowledge of the lives and achievements of some of these remarkable women. How many questions are you able to answer?

1. She spent fewer than two years in the country, yet she wrote a classic account of her travels in Upper Canada, made on her own, while her husband was busy in York. Who was she?

2. After the death of the youngest of her four children from drinking contaminated milk, Adelaide Hunter Hoodless devoted her life to educating mothers in home-making skills. In 1897, she founded what federation?

3. She has two monuments, one at Drummond Hill Cemetery, another at Queenston Heights. Although American-born, she aided the British forces. Her deed went unrewarded for forty-eight years. Who was she and what did she do?

4. Was it Emily G. Murphy or Nellie McClung who arranged the Mock Parliament in Winnipeg in 1914 to further the suffragette cause? Was it Nellie McClung or Emily G. Murphy who was appointed in Edmonton in 1916 the first woman police magistrate in the British Empire?

5. Emily Howard Stowe was a most persistent woman and, in 1880, became the first woman authorized to _____ in Canada. Three years later, her daughter, proving herself to be equally able, became the first woman to _____ in Canada.

6. Inspired by the Group of Seven, she returned to her paintings. Not only do her canvases depict totem poles different from those before or since, but her first book of reminiscences won the Governor General's Award for Literature. Who was this woman?

7. She defended, pretty well single-handedly, the small fortification on her

parents' seigneury on the south bank of the St. Lawrence. She held it against the attacking Iroquois, causing them to withdraw after two days. Name this heroic young woman.

156. Women's Firsts

It goes without saying that in politics women have been discriminated against. The cause of women's rights has been notably advanced by the persons whose names appear below. Yet despite the progress made by these women, no female has (as of 1983) yet served as governor general, prime minister, premier, or even Territorial commissioner. Match the accomplishment with the woman.

1. First woman elected to a provincial legislature, not only in Canada but in the entire British Empire.

    A. Cairine Wilson.

2. First woman elected to the House of Commons.

    B. Pauline McGibbon.

3. First woman elected to the House of Commons to serve in the Cabinet.

    C. Agnes Macphail.

4. First woman elected to the House of Commons to serve as Speaker.

    D. Louise C. McKinney.

5. First woman appointed to the Senate.

    E. Ellen Fairclough.

6. First woman to serve as lieutenant-governor.

    F. Pauline Jewett.

7. First woman to head a university, the institution being Simon Fraser University.

    G. Jeanne Sauvé.

157. Female Emancipation

1. In 1916, _____ became the first province to grant women the right to vote. In 1940, _____ became the last province to do so.

2. Five prominent women from Alberta petitioned the Supreme Court of Canada in what became known as the *Persons* Case. Six names appear below. Which name should not be included along with the other five?
   A. H. Edwards.
   B. N. McClung.
   C. L. McKinney.
   D. E. Murphy.
   E. I. Parlby.
   F. A. Persons.

3. Is the following statement true or false? The Supreme Court of Canada referred the *Persons* Case to the Judicial Committee of the Privy Council, which in 1929 rendered its decision on whether or not women were "qualified persons" for Senate appointment according to Section 24 of the BNA Act.

4. According to the decision of the Judicial Committee of the Privy Council, "The word persons includes —
   A. "Members of the female sex."
   B. "Members of the male and female sex."
   C. "Members of the Dominion of Canada."
   D. "All British subjects."

5. The judicial decision was a popular one, and as a result of the *Persons* Case:
   A. Three years later a woman was appointed to the Senate.
   B. One of the five Alberta women was appointed to the Senate.
   C. None of the five Alberta women was appointed to the Senate.
   D. The very next year a woman was appointed to the Senate.

---

158. Line of Work

Since the 1960s, women have become aware of their collective contribution to the world, of their leading contribution to the world of work. Here is a list of living Canadian women whose jobs keep them in the public eye. Match the names (on the left) with the phrases (on the right). The phrases are jargon or slang that suggest different lines of work.

1.	Doris Anderson.	A.	At the barre.
2.	Bertha Black.	B.	In the stacks.
3.	Madame Benoît.	C.	At the foundry.
4.	Barbara Frum.	D.	On mike.
5.	Phyllis Grosskurth.	E.	In print.
6.	Abby Hoffman.	F.	On the bench.
7.	Karen Kain.	G.	On key.
8.	Marian Kantaroff.	H.	On the masthead.
9.	Betty Kennedy.	I.	On cue.
10.	Margaret Laurence.	J.	At the starting-line.
11.	Catherine McKinnon.	K.	On camera.
12.	Kate Nelligan.	L.	In the brink.
13.	Cindy Nicholas.	M.	At the range.
14.	Jeanne Sauvé.	N.	In concert.
15.	Lois Marshall.	O.	On a point of order.

---

159. Outstanding Women

The talent, ability, and hard work of these women is not what makes them outstanding — at least not for this puzzle. What is remarkable is how *outstanding* they are in this puzzle, for their names do not appear to *stand out* in the maze of letters — unless one looks closely and methodically. There are two problems here. The first is to supply the last names of the ten women whose first names and professions are given in the list below. Then locate their last names in the maze. (The surnames appear horizontally or vertically — never diagonally or any other way. Names may share letters and intersect.) There is a bonus here, for the careful puzzler will find an eleventh name — in this case, the familiar form of the first name of a well-known personality.

1. Rosalie _____ (lawyer).
2. Margaret _____ (author).
3. Maureen _____ (contralto).
4. Dorothy _____ (poet).
5. Anne _____ (singer).

6. Sylvia _____ (economist).
7. Kate _____ (actress).
8. Veronica _____ (dancer).
9. Sylvia _____ (singer).
10. Joyce _____ (artist).

```
A  G  G  W  E  R  E  I  W  T  D  C
O  F  O  R  R  E  S  T  E  R  P  I
S  O  R  E  D  I  T  O  I  Q  Z  V
T  R  S  I  U  D  Z  K  L  J  O  A
Y  M  A  N  M  U  R  R  A  Y  S  B
S  A  B  P  O  R  M  H  N  T  A  L
O  G  E  A  T  W  O  O  D  E  V  S
N  G  L  I  V  E  S  A  Y  N  E  W
W  I  L  G  A  N  T  J  I  N  N  P
O  E  A  M  V  I  R  E  N  A  I  O
D  I  V  E  F  T  Y  S  O  N  E  V
G  Z  K  U  M  Z  O  W  O  T  Y  S
```

WORK

160. Associations

This is a series of questions on a serious subject — the right of free men and women to organize freely. This right, not easily won, could easily be lost. Answer as many of these questions as you can.

1. Not all unions are unions, of course. From the clues given, identify each of these non-unions.
   A. Great Britain's from 1801; Canada's to 1965.
   B. Borden's between 1917 and 1920.
   C. Toronto's from 6 August 1927.
   D. Duplessis's from 1935 on.

2. The motto of Canada's oldest printing association, the International Typographical Union, formed 1844, runs: "United to Support, Not Combined to _____."

3. There is a six-metre- (twenty-foot-) high statue of a miner in Springhill, _____, erected in honor of the miners who lost their lives in the Explosion of 1891. It was dedicated by the governor general and the prime minister. It is called "The _____ Miner."

4. The Fishermen's Protective Union was led by Sir William Ford _____ (1871-1938) of the Province of _____. In the words of the song, he boasted that he was "forty thousand strong."

5. In Calgary in 1919, workers formed the One Big Union to act as an industrial union, as distinct from the older _____ unions.

6. What is the difference between the CLC and the UIC?

7. What union, formed in 1963 as the result of a merger of two existing unions, became Canada's largest union? Does it represent federal government employees?

8. There was a one-day general strike of union members on 14 October 1976. One million union members took part to protest the Trudeau administration's

policy of wage controls as administered by the _____ Board. It was the first general strike on a national basis in Canada. What was it called?

9. In Europe the day to honor labor is May Day — the first of May. When is it in Canada?

---

161. Occupations

The object of this quiz is to remember or guess the occupation of a prominent Canadian. What is he or she famous for?

1. Phyllis Lambert is an architect, while Phyllis Gotlieb is a _____.
2. Robert Paul is a champion figure skater, while Paul Anka is a _____.
3. Joseph Howe was a journalist and statesman, while Josef Skvorecky is a _____.
4. Pierre Juneau is a telecommunications specialist, while Pierre Sévigny is a _____.
5. Johnny Wayne is a comedian, while Johnny Esaw is a _____.
6. Herbert Norman was a diplomat, while Norm Perry is a _____.
7. Joseph Bernier was an Arctic explorer, while Joseph MacInnis is a _____.
8. Charles Bruce was a poet and novelist, while his son Harry Bruce is a _____
9. Jules Léger was governor general, while his brother Paul-Emile Léger became _____.
10. Tom Thomson was a painter, while Kenneth Thomson is a _____.
11. Alfred Purdy is a poet, while Alfred Powis is a _____.
12. Edwin A. Goodman is a lawyer, while Jerry Goodis is a _____.
13. Marian Kantaroff is a sculptor, while Marian Hilliard was a _____.
14. Gilles Carle is a film-maker, while Gilles Vigneault is a _____.
15. The Marquess of Lorne was a governor general, while Lorne Pierce was a _____.
16. R.E. Knowles was a clergyman and newspaper columnist, while Stanley Knowles is a _____.
17. Marie-Claire Blais is a novelist, while Claire Haddad is a _____.
18. Barbara Amiel is a journalist, while Barbara Hamilton is a _____.
19. William Shatner is an actor, while William (Bill) Reid is a _____.
20. William E. Blatz was a child psychologist, while W.H. Blake was a _____.
21. Arthur Hailey is a bestselling novelist, while Arthur Maloney is a _____.
22. Dave Godfrey is a novelist and media specialist, while Dave Barrett is a _____.
23. Jan Drabek is a novelist and writer, while Jan Rubes is a _____.
24. Edward (Ned) A. Corbett was an educator, while Edwin (Ned) J. Pratt was a _____.
25. Audrey Thomas is a novelist, while Heather Thomson is a _____.
26. Joyce Wieland is an artist, while Joyce Davidson is a _____.
27. Lois Marshall is a singer, while Joyce Marshall is a _____.

---

162. Names in the News

All of these people are well known, at least in their own lines of work. Many of them have seen their names in the news in the 1980s. The idea is to fill in the blanks, and thus identify the occupations of these personalities.

1. If Paul Anka met Sylvanus Apps, a singer-composer would meet an _____.
2. If Roy Bonisteel met Conrad Black, a TV personality would meet a _____.
3. If Jean Chrétien met Heather Cooper, a _____ would meet an illustrator.
4. If Yves Deschamps met A.J. Diamond, a _____ would meet an architect.
5. If James Endicott met Sam Etcheverry, a spokesman for peace would meet a _____.
6. If Eugene Forsey met Victor Feldbrill, a constitutional expert would meet a _____.
7. If Avelino Gomez met Gratien Gélinas, a _____ would meet a theater personality.
8. If Abby Hoffman met Helen S. Hogg, a track star, runner would meet an _____.
9. If Punch Imlach met Elmer Iseler, a hockey coach would meet a _____.
10. If Don Jamieson met Greg Joy, a high commissioner would meet a _____.
11. If Harvey Kirck met Hugh Kenner, a _____ would meet a literary critic.
12. If Bora Laskin met Elmer Lach, a _____ would meet a hockey player.
13. If Brian Mulroney met Dennis McDermott, a politician would meet a _____.
14. If Phil Nimmons met Cindy Nicholas, a composer would meet a _____.
15. If Alanis Obomosawin met Bobby Orr, a folksinger would meet a _____.
16. If John Polanyi met Denis Potvin, a _____ would meet a hockey player.
17. If Wendy Quirk met Louis Quilico, a swimmer would meet a _____.
18. If George Ryga met Kate Reid, a _____ would meet an actress.
19. If Marlene Stewart Streit met Louis Siminovitch, a _____ would meet a physicist.
20. If John Turner met Kenneth Thomson, a _____ would meet a business executive.
21. If Tony Urquhart met Irv Ungerman, an artist would meet a _____.
22. If Jean Vanier met Gilles Vigneault, a _____ would meet a singer.
23. If Jack Webster met Austin Willis, a _____ would meet an actor.
24. If an employee of the XY Company met an employee of station XWA, a _____ would meet a radio broadcaster.
25. If Neil Young met Walter Yarwood, a _____ would meet a sculptor.
26. If Larry Zolf met Moses Znaimer, a _____ would meet a TV executive.

163. Through Foreign Eyes

Canada has attracted leading British and American authors who have, in their personal letters and autobiographies, preserved their impressions of Canada and their experiences with Canadians. Here are eight passages from the writings of eminent authors, followed by the names of three authors with the dates of composition. Choose the correct writer.

1. "I see no argument for the union of Canada with the United States. There is excellent feeling between the two countries, but they could no more join at this period of their history than a great oak could combine with a well-rooted pine to make one tree. The roots of each are far too deep. It is impossible."
   A. Charles Dickens, 1842.
   B. Sir Arthur Conan Doyle, 1914.
   C. Oscar Wilde, 1882.

2. "Canadian girls are so pretty it is a relief to see a plain one now and then."
   A. Rupert Brooke, 1913.
   B. Mark Twain, 1883.
   C. Walt Whitman, 1880.

3. "Canada has held, and always will retain, a foremost place in my remembrance. Few Englishmen are prepared to find it what it is. Advancing quietly . . . it is full of hope and promise."
   A. Rupert Brooke, 1913.
   B. Charles Dickens, 1842.
   C. Rudyard Kipling, 1907.

4. "I am having charming audiences, you will be glad to hear; the Canadians are very appreciative people, but it is a great fight in this commercial age to plead the cause of Art."
   A. Rupert Brooke, 1913.
   B. Walt Whitman, 1880.
   C. Oscar Wilde, 1882.

5. "Lord, Lord — I've not really given the Canadians much chance yet. But my impression *is* that they have all the faults of the Americans, and not their one lovely and redeeming virtue, 'hospitality.' "

   A. Rupert Brooke, 1913.
   B. Rudyard Kipling, 1907.
   C. Oscar Wilde, 1882.

6. "Canada is one of the several places where, thanks to the valour and wisdom of our forefathers and to the labour and self-denial of our brethren elsewhere, a certain place has been secured in which a man may sit down and grow strong and wise against whatever chances may befall him."

   A. Sir Arthur Conan Doyle, 1914.
   B. Rudyard Kipling, 1907.
   C. Walt Whitman, 1880.

7. "We are off, off into Toronto Bay (soon the wide expanse and cool breezes of Lake Ontario). . . . Goodbye, Toronto, with your memories of a very lively and agreeable visit."

   A. Rupert Brooke, 1913.
   B. Mark Twain, 1883.
   C. Walt Whitman, 1880.

8. "Niagara Falls is the most beautiful object in the world."

   A. Charles Dickens, 1842
   B. Henry James, 1883.
   C. Mark Twain, 1883.

---

164. Canadians Abroad

Canada is known around the world for its hockey and wheat, Inuit and Indians, peacekeeping and plenty, but not for very much more. Yet in certain countries and parts of the world, through the good actions of individual Canadians, there is a greater appreciation of things Canadian. In this set of questions, select the country in which the individual made his most outstanding contribution.

1. Jean Vanier, son of Governor General Georges Vanier, established homes for the mentally handicapped. He called the first one L'Arche in 1964 and located it in:

   A. Angola.
   B. Belgium.
   C. France.
   D. Switzerland.

2. William Jones, a member of the Canadian Black Watch in World War I, enlisted in the RAF in World War II, parachuted into a European country, and acted as liaison officer for the Partisans and the British War Office in 1943-44. To the Germans he was known as "the phantom general of the Balkans," and to the British Foreign Office as "Lawrence of _____." He was subsequently decorated for his resourcefulness and bravery.

   A. Bulgaria.
   B. Hungary.
   C. Romania.
   D. Yugoslavia.

3. This Toronto-based holding company, with many international interests, at one time controlled almost all the light and power utilities of a foreign country. Its involvement with this Latin American country dates back to the building of a tramway in 1899. Both the country's and the company's economies grew, side by side. Now the company is gradually withdrawing. The country is:

A. Argentina.
B. Brazil.
C. Columbia.
D. Mexico.

4. Norman Bethune was an idealistic medical doctor who organized the world's first mobile blood-transfusion service. Sometime later he died of an infection contracted while performing a medical operation not far from a field of battle, and became a hero to almost one-quarter of the world's population. He pioneered his mobile blood-transfusion service in:

A. Belgium.
B. China.
C. Spain.
D. Russia.

5. Joe Boyle was the "King of the Klondike" before heading for Europe where, in 1917, he made an attempt to save the lives of the Tzar's family. Thereafter he became a confidant of an Eastern European queen. He was a power behind a throne, and in his day he was dubbed: "The Uncrowned King of _____."

A. Bulgaria.
B. Czechoslovakia.
C. Romania.
D. Yugoslavia.

6. Davidson Black was an anthropologist with the Royal Ontario Museum who uncovered the skull and bones of a man he believed to be a million years old. The remains, dug up in 1929, disappeared in 1941 and have never been recovered. One of Black's associates was Teilhard de Chardin, the philosopher. They worked together in:

A. China.
B. Kenya.
C. South Yemen.
D. Tanzania.

7. Max Saltsman, when he was a member of Parliament, submitted a private member's bill in 1974. It was an act respecting a proposed association between Canada and a British colony in the Caribbean which comprises thirty-odd islands, only six of which are inhabited, total population about six thousand. The association would give Canada "a place in the sun." The islands are:

A. Saint Christopher-Nevis-Anguilla.
B. Saint Pierre and Miquelon.
C. Falkland Islands.
D. Turks and Caicos Islands.

8. Peter Dmytruk, a young flier of Ukrainian background from Wynyard, Sask., was shot down by German occupation troops at a small village somewhere in Europe. He joined the Resistance but was caught and killed in 1943. His body is buried in this village, which has been twinned with the town of

Wynyard, where he is still remembered as "Pierre le Canadien." The town and country are:

A. Berne, Switzerland.
B. Hainaut, Belgium.
C. Martres-de-Veyre, France.
D. Monte Carlo, Monaco.

9. Stephan Gudmundsson Stephansson was born in Iceland but emigrated to the Canadian North West. In 1889 he settled in what is now Alberta and lived there, latterly at Innisfail, until his death in 1927. His farmhouse is now a provincial museum devoted to his work. During his lifetime he was recognized as Iceland's leading bard for, in the words of one critic, his lyrics were "unsurpassed by any other Icelandic poet since the Middle Ages." His numerous books were published in Iceland's capital, which is:

A. Bergen.
B. Copenhagen.
C. Godthaab.
D. Reykjavik.

10. Cyrus Eaton, a native of Nova Scotia and an owner of Ungava Iron Ores Co. Ltd., decided that Albert Einstein and Bertrand Russell were right and that what the world urgently required, at the height of the Cold War, was a top-level conference on science and world peace. He brought together twenty-two leading scientists from the communist and non-communist world in the first of a series of meetings that continue to this day. The first, ground-breaking meeting was held in July 1957 at:

A. Cleveland, Ohio, U.S.A.
B. Moscow, Russia, U.S.S.R.
C. Pugwash, N.S., Canada
D. Washington, D.C., U.S.A.

11. Paul-Emile Léger, a cardinal in the Church of Rome, after seventeen years as Archbishop of Montreal, stepped down in Centennial year to devote the rest of his life to missionary work. He became a priest at a medical mission devoted to lepers in:

A. Cameroon.
B. Gabon.
C. Sudan.
D. Tanzania.

12. John G. Diefenbaker was the recipient of an unusual honor. Diefenbaker Parkway was named in his honor. It runs through a forest of five million trees, called Canada Park, which occupies the most densely populated part of this country. Prior to 1970, the 3,038-hectare (7,500-acre) park was nothing but rocky ground. The country is:

A. Chile.
B. Israel.
C. South Korea.
D. West Germany.

165. Farewell!

Farewells to the reader follow in both official languages, in two of the native tongues, and in Esperanto. Match the words of farewell (left) with their respective languages (right).

1. Adíaŭ!
2. Adieu!
3. Assutnai!
4. Goodbye!
5. K'gah waubmin meenwauh!

A. Algonkian.
B. English.
C. Esperanto.
D. French.
E. Inuktitut.

1. Hail!

1. A. The Cree form of greeting.
2. E. The gesture of acknowledgment in the Inuktitut language as spoken by the Inuit of northern Quebec; somewhat similarly used across the Northwest Territories is *tavvauvutit*.
3. B. The English interjection of surprise, as in greeting, has such variants as hallo, hollo, hullo, etc.
4. D. An all-purpose French interjection.
5. C. Esperanto is the most widely adopted, artificially created "world language."

2. Abbreviations

1. Associateship, Royal Conservatory of Music.
2. Canadian Armed Forces.
3. Canadian Broadcasting Corporation.
4. Canada. (Official abbreviation for foreign automobile license-plate registration, etc.)
5. Canadian Labour Congress.
6. Canadian National.
7. Canadian Pacific.
8. Canadian Radio-Television and Telecommunications Commission.
9. Canadian Television Network.
10. Fellow of the Royal Society of Canada.
11. New Democratic Party. (Formerly the CCF — Co-operative Commonwealth Federation.)
12. National Hockey League.
13. Order of Canada.
14. Queen's Counsel.
15. Société royale du Canada (French equivalent of FRSC).
16. Upper Canada College.
17. W5, the title of a long-running CTV-TV news and public-affairs show, cleverly alludes to the journalist's five W's — who, what, when, where, and why.

3. Acronyms

1. Colleges of Applied Arts and Technology.
2. CANada-Deuterium-Uranium (or nuclear) reactor.
3. *Collèges d'Enseignement Général et Professionnel* — the equivalent in Quebec of the CAATs.
4. Canadian International Development Agency.
5. Canadian Union of Public Employees.
6. Canadian University Service Overseas.
7. Foreign Investment Review Agency.
8. North Atlantic Treaty Organization.
9. North American Air (Aerospace) Defence Command.

4. Agricultural Statistics

1. A.
2. D.
3. B.
4. C.
5. B.
6. Ontario.
7. C.
8. Alberta, Manitoba, and Saskatchewan.
9. High-quality red spring wheat.
10. Saskatchewan.
11. C.
12. D.

5. The Greatest Good

1. Prince Edward Island.
2. Dairy.
3. Land of rape and honey.
4. The apple.
5. The potato.
6. Prince Edward Island.
7. Pears, peaches, cherries, and plums.
8. Niagara Peninsula.
9. British Columbia. Okanagan Valley. (The Fraser Valley produces raspberries and strawberries.)
10. No. There is a separate Ontario Wheat Producers' Marketing Board.
11. Sir Charles E. Saunders.

12. C.
13. C.
14. B.
15. True.
16. True
17. False.

6. Symbology

1. The Crown is emblematic of the relationship of the Canadian Armed Forces to the sovereign as Queen of Canada.
2. The maple leaves symbolize Canada; the ten leaves represent the ten provinces.
3. These three devices — the fouled anchor, the crossed swords, and the flying eagle — represent the three universal elements in which the Canadian Armed Forces operate in carrying out their mission.
4. Blue suggests loyalty and devotion.

7. Canadian Armed Forces

1. Canada became the first country to bring about a unification of its three armed forces — the army, the navy, and the air force. This marked the creation of the Canadian Armed Forces.
2. The Canadian Militia.
3. Corvettes had either "Flower" or "Castle" designations.
4. *Sic Itur ad Astra* (Such is the Pathway to the Stars). That is the Air Command motto. The motto that appears on the Air Operations Badge is *Per Ardua ad Astra* (Through Adversity to the Stars).
5. Canadian (or Cadet) Officers' Training Corps. Its function is now served by the Canadian Armed Forces Cadets.
6. Chief of Defence Staff. Ministry of National Defence.
7. A. Brigade.
   B. Squadrons.
   C. Yes.
8. A. The Argus is a patrol plane; so Air Command, or air force.
   B. The Centurion is a tank; so Mobile Command, or army.
   C. The Leopard is also a tank; so Mobile Command, or army.
   D. The Sea King is a helicopter; so Marine Command, or navy.
   E. The Starfighter is a fighter plane; so Air Command, or air force.
9. Lahr.
10. Shearwater. Nova Scotia.
11. Collège Militaire Royal, Saint-Jean, Que. Royal Roads Military College, Hatley Park, near Esquimalt, B.C.
12. A. Pine Tree Line.
    B. Mid-Canada Line.
    C. DEW Line.
13. The Snowbirds. It was named after the song sung by Anne Murray.
14. Camp X is the code name of a training camp and communications center for guerrilla warfare and intelligence operations during the Second World War. Located outside Pickering, Ont., and given a cover by the CBC, it was run by Sir William Stephenson. Station M faked and forged documents.
15. With the Suez Crisis of 1956, Canada committed service and supply troops to many United Nations "peacekeeping" missions.

8. Popular Paintings

1. E.   5. B.
2. G.   6. C.
3. F.   7. D.
4. A.

9. Group of Eleven?

2. A.J. Casson. (A late member.)
3. Lionel LeMoine Fitzgerald. (A late member.)
5. Edwin H. Holgate. (A late member.)
10. Tom Thomson. (Never a member, having died before the Group was founded.)

10. Arts and Crafts

1. Joyce Weiland.
2. Thomson.
3. The Regina Five.
4. Hunt.
5. Colville.
6. Partridge.
7. Painters Eleven.
8. *Fraktur* is a kind of black-letter, ornate calligraphy.
9. *Refus Global* (Global Refusal).
10. Norval Morrisseau.

11. Pratt. Newfoundland.
12. Louis-Philippe was the father, Louis-Henri the son.
13. His model cows are especially charming.
14. "Northwest Indians." The French anthropologist was particularly impressed with Haida and Kwakiutl poles and masks.
15. Japan supplied the technique — and perhaps some of the vision — through the good offices of James Houston.
16. "Woman."

11. Comic Art

1. Elias Disney, Walt's father, was born in Goderich, Ont.
2. B.
3. "Prince Valiant in King Arthur's Court."
4. A. Joe Shuster wrote the script; Jerry Siegel drew it.
   B. The *Daily Planet* is modeled on the *Toronto Daily Star*.
   C. Krypton.
5. "Dick Tracy."
6. Brownies.
7. Ben Wicks.
8. Aislin, the pen name of Terry Mosher.
9. A. ii.
   B. iii.
   C. i.

12. Photography

1. William Notman.
2. Yousuf Karsh.
3. Richard Harrington.
4. Roloff Benny.
5. *Between Friends/Entre Amis*.
6. Freeman Patterson.

13. Winners All!

1. B.		8. B.
2. C.		9. A.
3. B.		10. B.
4. B.		11. A.
5. B.		12. C.
6. C.		13. A.
7. B.		14. Could be A., B., or C.

14. Nobel Laureates

1. True. (Banting shared the monetary reward with Charles H. Best, Macleod with Dr. J.B. Collip.)
2. Lester B. Pearson, later prime minister.
3. C.
4. Right.
5. False. (Although born in Canada — at Lachine, Que. — Bellow became a naturalized American.)
6. From the crest of Signal Hill, St. John's, Nfld., with an aerial flown from a kite, Marconi received the first transatlantic wireless message, 12 December 1901.
7. Sir Ernest Rutherford and Frederick Soddy.
8. Dr. Khorana worked on cell synthesis at the British Columbia Research Council between 1952 and 1959 and continued that work at the University of Wisconsin.

15. Residences of Renown

1. I. (Port Hope, Ont.)
2. K. (Toronto)
3. P. (Montreal)
4. H. (Quebec City)
5. O. (Near Brantford, Ont.)
6. U. (Toronto; lieutenant-governor's residence, now levelled.)
7. T. (Windsor, N.S.)
8. J. (Hamilton, Ont.)
9. Q. (Victoria)
10. L. (Ottawa)
11. N. (Ottawa)
12. E. (London, Ont.)
13. F. (Ottawa)
14. G. (London, Ont.)
15. S. (Oshawa, Ont.)
16. R. (Montreal)
17. D. (Ottawa; official residence of the governor general.)
18. M. (Quebec City; official residence of British governors, now levelled.)
19. C. (Ottawa; official residence of the leader of the opposition.)
20. A. (Ottawa; official residence of the prime minister.)
21. B. (Mount Uniak, N.S.)

16. Chateaux in Canada

1. The Château Clique is the popular name for the appointed officials in

Lower Canada before 1841; they met at the Château St. Louis.

2. Museum.
3. Quebec City. (It also overlooks the St. Lawrence River.)
4. Wine and winery.
5. CP.
6. Ottawa.
7. CP.
8. The early French governors of New France and of British North America.
9. Montreal.

17. What Building Is This?

1. Parliament Buildings, Ottawa, Ontario. (Ontario Ministry of Industry and Tourism)
2. Algonquin Hotel, St. Andrews, New Brunswick. (Tourism New Brunswick)
3. Bessborough Hotel, Saskatoon, Saskatchewan. (Saskatchewan Government Photograph)
4. Confederation Centre, Charlottetown, Prince Edward Island. (P.E.I. Tourism)
5. Roosevelt Summer Home, Campobello Island, New Brunswick. (Tourism New Brunswick)
6. Banff Springs Hotel, Banff, Alberta. (Travel Alberta)
7. Château Frontenac, Quebec City, Quebec. (Gouvernement du Québec)
8. Shakespearean Festival Theatre, Stratford, Ontario. (Ontario Ministry of Industry and Tourism)
9. Province House, Halifax, Nova Scotia. (Nova Scotia Communications)
10. B.C. Place, Vancouver, British Columbia. (B.C. Ministry of Tourism)
11. Basilica, Sainte-Anne-de-Beaupré, Quebec. (Gouvernement du Québec)
12. Cabot Tower, Signal Hill, St. John's, Newfoundland. (Nfld. Tourist Services Division)
13. CN Tower, Toronto, Ontario. (Ontario Ministry of Industry and Tourism)

18. Architects All

1. G.
2. J.
3. K.
4. M.
5. O.
9. L.
10. B.
11. N.
12. A.
13. I.

6. H.
7. D. or E.
8. F.
14. E. or D.
15. C.

19. Memorable Memorials

1. "Gassy Jack" may be viewed in Vancouver's Gastown.
2. Champlain's statue rises above Couchiching Beach Park, Orillia, Ont.
3. Golden Boy rises 240 feet above the City of Winnipeg.
4. Sir Galahad's statue commemorates the heroism of Henry Albert Harper and stands at the foot of Parliament Hill, Ottawa.
5. The effigy of Josiah Flintabbaty Flonatin (nicknamed Flin Flon), the hero of J.E. Preston-Muddock's dime novel The Sunless City, gave his name to Flin Flon, Man., where grateful citizens had the statue designed by Al Capp and erected.

20. Misnomers

1. "Peace, order, and good government" is what the BNA Act provides. The American Constitution guarantees "life, liberty, and the pursuit of happiness."
2. As there are ten provinces, nine cannot gang up against two. (Occasionally nine predominantly English-speaking provinces do gang up against Quebec, the single predominantly French-speaking province.)
3. The Baby Bonus is the popular name of the Family Allowance.
4. The British North America (not American) Act.
5. Multiculturalism and bilingualism.
6. The Canada (not Canadian) Council.
7. There are two northern territories.
8. North of Sixty (not Sixty-five) is the parallel that marks the southern boundary of the Northwest Territories and the Yukon Territory.
9. Daylight Saving (not spending) Time.
10. Trail of '98 (not '88) refers to the Yukon Gold Rush of 1898.
11. This may be so, but the classic expression is Sir Wilfrid Laurier's "The twentieth century belongs to Canada."
12. The Forty-eighth Parallel divides North

from South Korea; the parallel that separates Canada and the United States is the Forty-ninth.

13. There is no Western Standard Time, but there is Pacific Standard Time.

14. "Apprehended insurrection" is a phrase associated with the War Measures Act which permits the imposition of martial law during a time of peace.

15. There are four Atlantic Provinces (Nfld., N.S., N.B., P.E.I.) but only three Maritime Provinces (excluding Nfld.).

16. There are four Western Provinces (B.C., Alta., Sask., Man.) but only three Prairie Provinces (excluding B.C.).

17. There are thirty-six Fathers of Confederation, and while Sir John A. Macdonald became the first prime minister, there is no single Father of Confederation.

21. Fun With Words

1. LAVAL. (Laval University — l'Université de Laval — is located in Quebec City.)

2. A. MAPLE SUGAR.
   B. ALEXANDER GRAHAM BELL.
   C. ESKIMO.
   D. NOVA SCOTIA AND PRINCE EDWARD ISLAND.

3. HOMES is both an acronym and a mnemonic if you remembered (or deduced) that the five letters stand for the names of the five Great Lakes. (H—Huron; O—Ontario; M—Michigan; E—Erie; S—Superior.)

4. Adanac is appropriately Canadian because it is Canada backwards.

22. The Force

1. North West Mounted Police.

2. Royal North West Mounted Police.

3. Ontario and Quebec.

4. *Maintiens le droit*. The motto in English is "Uphold the Right."

5. B.

6. The RCMP has been called "The Barnburners" since May 1972 when, to combat revolutionary terrorism in Quebec, it had a hand in burning down the barn at Ste. Anne de la Rochelle, near Montreal, used as a meeting place for the FLQ and the American Black Panthers.

7. La Gendarmerie royale du Canada.

8. A. The Red Serge is a reference to the red jackets made of heavy wool serge worn by the Mounties.
   B. Scarlet and Stetson is a reference to the red jackets and the broad-brimmed hats worn by the Mounties.

9. Sergeant Renfrew (and his dog Cuddles) is a character created by the comedian Dave Broadfoot. Renfrew may bungle all his investigations, yet he usually manages to "get his man," if not his horse.

23. Innumerable Numbers

1. A strain of wheat fabled for its hardness.

2. Title of Hugh MacLennan's famous novel about the French and English.

3. First Canadian postage stamp, 1851.

4. Roger Bannister ran the "miracle mile" at the British Empire and Commonwealth Games, Vancouver, 1954.

5. "Five Basic Exercises for Men" developed by the RCAF in the 1950s.

6. Six Nations Confederacy and Reserve, Grand River, Ont.

7. Massacre of Seven Oaks, 1816.

8. Title of a people's play written for a Communist group and produced in Toronto to much controversy in 1931.

9. Slogan adopted by the Toronto Trades Assembly, 1872.

10. Title of a book of oral history about the Depression by Barry Broadfoot, and the musical play based on it.

11. Nickname of Henry Fuller Davis, who once prospected a twelve-foot claim.

12. Number of valiant men who, with Adam Dollard, defended Long Sault, 1660.

13. Title of a naturalistic novel by Ringuet.

14. List of grievances and recommendations drawn by Louis-Joseph Papineau in the Rebellion of 1837.

15. Reference to the Chilkoot Pass scaled by prospectors during the Klondike Gold Rush of 1898.

16. The Company of One Hundred Associates, formed to colonize New France, 1627.

17. Major highway across southern Ontario, officially called the Macdonald-Cartier Freeway.
18. Dates on the device of the Mackenzie-Papineau Battalion.
19. Collective name for the islands of eastern Georgian Bay.
20. Title of an influential report on disturbed children, 1970.
21. Name of a society to provide decent burials for destitute and friendless ex-servicemen.

24. Capitalists

1. T.	11. D.		
2. M.	12. H.		
3. K.	13. E.		
4. J.	14. L.		
5. N.	15. I.		
6. B.	16. R.		
7. F.	17. P.		
8. O.	18. S.		
9. A.	19. C.		
10. Q.	20. G.		

25. Corporate Identities

1. Bombardier Inc.
2. George Weston Limited.
3. GWG Inc. The initials stand for Great Western Garment Company Ltd.
4. C-I-L Inc.
5. Téléglobe Canada is the Crown corporation which maintains and operates Canada's external telecommunications services (telegraph, telephone, telex, and other international transmissions).
6. Petro-Canada.
7. Roy Thomson, founder of Thomson Newspapers Limited.
8. H.R. MacMillan, a founder of MacMillan Bloedel Ltd.

26. Inspired Commercials

1. Speedy Muffler King.
2. CCM.
3. T. Eaton Co. Ltd.'s original catalogue guarantee.
4. Carling O'Keefe Black Label Lager Beer.
5. Dominion Stores Ltd.
6. Loblaws Ltd.
7. Red Rose Tea.
8. DOFASCO.
9. G.H. Wood & Co. Ltd.
10. Provincial Milk Marketing Boards.

27. Higher Learning

1. L.	10. B.
2. E.	11. D.
3. N.	12. F.
4. A.	13. G.
5. M.	14. K.
6. Q.	15. H.
7. C.	16. I.
8. P.	17. J.
9. O.	

28. Worlds of Learning

1. The Antigonish Movement. (Part of the movement is the Coady International Institute.)
2. Frontier College.
3. Father Athol Murray founded Notre Dame College, now called Athol Murray College of Notre Dame.
4. Khaki College.
5. Canadian Chautauqua.
6. Canadian University Service Overseas (CUSO).
7. National Farm Radio Forum. Sometimes abbreviated to "Farm Forum," it had an urban counterpart in "Citizens' Forum."
8. Pearson College of the Pacific.

29. Mammal-Watching

1. True.
2. The Alaskan brown bear is tallest, followed by the polar bear, the grizzly bear, and the black bear.
3. True.
4. High.
5. Fox.
6. B. and C.
7. True.
8. A specie of bat common throughout Canada and the United States.
9. Beaver.
10. B.
11. Correct as stated.
12. True.
13. Yes, the statement is true, except that both caribou are being overhunted.

14. True.
15. False. It is white in color, though the young are bluish gray.
16. Narwhal.

---

30. Flower-Watching

For each flower, the common name or names are given, along with the botanical name.

1. C. Great White Trillium. *Trillium grandiflorum.*
2. A. Moccasin Flower; Stemless Lady's Slipper; Pink Lady's Slipper. *Cypripedium acaule.*
3. B. Prairie Crocus; Pasque Flower. *Anemone patens.*
4. B. Ox-eye Daisy; Marguerite. *Chrysanthemum leucanthemum.*
5. C. Wolf Willow; Silverberry. *Elaeagnus commutata.*
6. C. Purple Mountain Saxifrage. *Saxifraga oppositifolia.*
7. B. Fragrant White Water Lily. *Nymphaea odorata.*
8. B. Pitcher Plant. *Sarracenia purpurea.*

---

31. Bird-Watching

Note: The common name in English appears first, followed by the common name in French, followed by the scientific name in Latin.

1. Snowy Owl. Le harfang des neiges. *Nytea scandiaca.*
2. Common Crow. La corneille américaine. *Corvus brachyrhynchos.*
3. Song Sparrow. Le pinson chanteur. *Melospiza melodia.*
4. Common Loon. Le huart à collier. *Gavia immer.*
5. Robin. Le merle américain. *Turdus migratorius.*
6. Blue Jay. Le geai bleu. *Cyanocitta cristata.*
7. *Cardinal. Le cardinal. Richmondena cardinalis.*
8. Ruffed Grouse. La gelinotte huppée. *Bonasa umbellus.*
9. Great Blue Heron. Le grand héron bleu. *Ardea herodias.*
10. Canada Goose. La bernache canadienne. *Branta canadensis.*

---

32. Fish-Watching

1. Newfoundland.
2. Cod.
3. Salmon.
4. Sockeye, Coho, Spring, Pink, Chum.
5. Great Lakes.
6. The declaration of an exclusive economic zone extending 200 nautical miles (320 km).
7. "rivers."

---

33. Knock On Wood

1. A. 7%. The statement is true.
2. True.
3. C. 37%.
4. A. Coniferous trees are those that have needlelike or scalelike leaves (conifers).
   B. Deciduous trees are those that have broadleafs in contrast to the conifers.
   C. More are deciduous. Of the 140 native tree species, 109 are deciduous, and only 31 are coniferous.
5. A. Hardwoods are deciduous.
   B. Softwoods are coniferous.
6. Douglas-fir, Jack Pine, and Sitka Spruce are coniferous. Yellow birch, Sugar Maple, and White Oak are deciduous.
7. False. More Spruce trees are marketed than Douglas-fir trees.
8. Sudbury.

---

34. Banking

1. Bank of Montreal.
2. Bank of Canada.
3. Royal Bank of Canada.
4. A. Royal Bank of Canada.
   B. Canadian Imperial Bank of Commerce.
   C. Bank of Montreal.
   D. Bank of Nova Scotia.
   E. Toronto-Dominion Bank.
5. Trust companies.
6. A credit union.
7. Kenneth Carter.
8. "My Financial Career."

---

35. Coins and Stamps

1. Royal Canadian Mint. Crown Corporation. Winnipeg. Master of the Mint.

2. Caught without a new die, the old one was reused and a raised dot was added under the date "1936." Hence the names "Dot Penny" and "Dot Dime." These are now valuable collectors' items.

3. Unshaded portions of Queen Elizabeth's hair created the illusion there was an ugly face behind her ear. New plates were prepared with a redone coiffure which eliminated the apparition. Thus the hirsute devil was banished!

4. Benjamin Franklin. Quebec City. Prepaid. Any or all of: The Province of Canada (present-day Quebec and Ontario); Nova Scotia; New Brunswick; Vancouver Island; British Columbia.

5. Beaver. Pence (or pennies). Three Penny Beaver (or three Pence Beaver). Sandford Fleming.

6. Red. "---than Has Been."

7. Princess Elizabeth (later Queen). A flaw in the engraving plate produced a tear-drop effect under the eye of the young Princess, giving the illusion that she was weeping.

8. This was the airmail policy, by which air delivery would be made of all possible first-class mail.

9. Postal code. Crown Corporation.

36. Name That Monster

1. Windigo. The name of the Algonkian demon of the woods is sometimes spelled Wendigo.

2. D'Sonoqua. There are many spellings for this fearsome female whose image was once painted by Emily Carr.

3. Sasquatch. The Squamish "hairy man" is also known as Bigfoot in the United States, and the Yeti in Nepal.

4. Thunderbird. The immense winged being of the Ojibway and West Coast Indians.

5. Sedna. The Inuit fear "the spirit of waters."

6. Ogopogo. The fabulous sea serpent of Lake Okanagan in the Penticton Valley of British Columbia is known as Ogopogo. Manitoba has its Manipogo, Ontario its Igopogo, New Brunswick its Lake Utopia Monster, etc.

37. Folk Songs

1. "Un Canadien Errant." (The title is twice repeated.)

2. Newfoundland. Wolf. "An Anti-Confederation Song."

3. rant. roar. "The Ryans and the Pittmans."

4. "Farewell to Nova Scotia." (The title begins the verse.)

5. "Peter Emberley." (The title turns up in the initial line.)

6. fraud. "Life in a Prairie Shack."

7. Soiree. "The Kelligrews Soiree."

8. Red River Valley. "The Red River Valley."

38. Atlantic Dishes

1.	E.	7.	D.
2.	I.	8.	H.
3.	A.	9.	C.
4.	B.	10.	F.
5.	L.	11.	J.
6.	G.	12.	K.

39. Drink Up!

1. Screech is a low-grade rum.

2. Winnipeg goldeye is a dish, Calgary red-eye is a drink. The dish is a tasty freshwater fish of the shad family, usually smoked. The drink is equal amounts of beer and tomato juice. (Purists will note that another favorite dish in Calgary is Beef and "Red Eye" — roasted prime rib and baked red kidney beans.)

3. Boxes. Afternoon. Victoria.

4. W.A.C. Bennett.

5. Niagara.

6. Baby Duck.

7. Woodstock.

8. Moosemilk is slang for a homebrew or for a drink that combines rum with a mixture of milk and cream.

9. V.O. stands for "Very Old." The phrase means, roughly, "None Better."

10. Blended. Alberta.

11. Walkerville, Ont. (A district of Windsor, Ont.) Canadian Club.

12. Crush. Honeydew.

13. Canada Dry Ginger Ale.

14. Blue.

15. A. Newfoundland.
    B. Maritimes, especially Nova Scotia and New Brunswick.
    C. Alberta.
    D. Maritimes, especially Nova Scotia and New Brunswick.
    E. Northern Ontario.
    F. British Columbia.
    G. Manitoba.
16. *Chimo!*

40. Eat Up!

1. Cheese. Quebec.
2. Yakallo is a cross between the buffalo and the yak. The experiment was tried in Alberta in the 1930s.
3. True.
4. Cheddar. Colby.
5. Edible (or at least chewable) was the company's bubble gum; collectable were its bubble-gum cards.
6. Export ''A.''
7. McIntosh. McIntosh Red.
8. Canola.
9. Ganong. Ganong Bros. Limited.
10. C.
11. New Brunswick.
12. Dulse.
13. Lethbridge.
14. Corn Syrup.
15. C.
16. True.
17. True.
18. Believed to be true.
19. Dr. Huntsman was a pioneer in the fast freezing of foods, a process employed in the preserving of fish by Birdseye.
20. Sunwheat.
21. Dried strips of caribou, moose, or other game.
22. Laura Secord chocolates. Farmer is associated with the American War of Independence, Secord with the Anglo-Canadian side of the War of 1812.

41. Going Places

1. Colombie-Britannique.
2. Nouveau-Brunswick.
3. Terre-Neuve.
4. Territoires du Nord-Ouest.
5. Nouvelle-Écosse.

6. Île du Prince-Edouard.
7. La Province du Québec.
8. Yukon.

42. How Fluent Is Your French?

1. S'il vous plaît.
2. Merci.
3. Pourquoi?
4. Comment ça va?
5. Qui est-ce?
6. Au revoir.
7. Bonsoir.
8. Quelle heure est-il?
9. Peut-être.
10. Bien sûr.
11. Vraiment!
12. Écoute bien.
13. Félicitations!
14. Enfin!
15. Bravo!
16. Je t'aime.
17. Voici la salle de bain.
18. Défense de fumer.
19. Mesdames et messieurs.
20. Dépêche-toi.
21. Réveille-toi.
22. Bonne chance!
23. C'est un secret.
24. Il était une fois . . .
25. C'est difficile.
26. Ne pleure pas.
27. Je comprends.
28. Calme-toi.
29. Va-t'en.
30. Je suis bilingue.

43. Bilingual Buying

1. Peanut butter creme cookies.
2. Raspberry jam.
3. Automatic dishwasher detergent.
4. Macaroni and cheese dinner.
5. Paper towels.
6. Pork and beans.
7. Quick oats.
8. Tomato juice.
9. Butterscotch ripple ice cream.
10. Pancake mix.
11. Facial tissues.
12. Window cleaner.
13. Bathroom tissue.
14. Ground black pepper.
15. Garlic powder.
16. Apple sauce.
17. Puffed rice.
18. Golden corn syrup.
19. Pure white vinegar.
20. Thousand Island dressing.

44. How Fluent Is Your English?

1. Dead end.
2. No passing.
3. Help!
4. Out of gas.
5. Detour.

6. Bridge under repair.
7. Do not enter.
8. One way.
9. Yield.
10. Stop.

---

45. General Questions

1. Sir Wilfrid Laurier, Louis St. Laurent, Pierre Elliott Trudeau.
2. "The Ballad of Springhill" was inspired by the Springhill, N.S., mining disaster.
3. John G. Diefenbaker.
4. Vineland. Wineland. L'Anse au Meadows, Nfld.
5. Rupert's Land.
6. The polecat.
7. James Montgomery.
8. A missionary, clergyman, minister, or priest.
9. The Rush-Bagot Agreement of 1817.
10. A narrow channel between an island and the mainland, or between two islands.
11. Voltaire.
12. "In the bedrooms of the nation."
13. Lake Champlain.
14. League for Social Reconstruction.
15. Health and Welfare Canada.
16. Santa's postal code is H0H 0H0.
17. A kit.
18. Engineering.
19. Peter Puck.
20. Super Constellation.
21. "In a hierarchy every employee tends to rise to his level of incompetence."
22. International Civil Aviation Organization.
23. Pierre Elliott Trudeau, Jean Marchand, Gerard Pelletier.
24. A sash with an arrow-head design of traditional manufacture.
25. Multiple Unit Residential Building, a tax-shelter definition.
26. The Trans-Canada Highway.
27. Boston Bruins.
28. Toronto.
29. New Brunswick.
30. The Déné Nation.
31. Mercury had poisoned the fish; the waters were polluted.
32. Ice hockey.
33. 264.
34. The Royal Canadian Air Force.
35. 5BX (Basic Exercises) is for men, 10BX for women.
36. Ungava.
37. Sniderman.
38. A quarter mile is longer.
39. Samuel de Champlain.
40. An inukshut.
41. Quebec.
42. Terry Fox.
43. The BNA Act, 1867.
44. *Maclean's*.
45. A deep blueberry pie.
46. Sir Arthur Currie.
47. Stephen Leacock.
48. Uncle Tom.
49. Fort Rouillé.
50. To the right.
51. Manitoba.
52. Massive power blackout.
53. The elk.
54. Asbestos, or Asbestosville.
55. Karen Kain and Frank Augustyn.
56. Don Shebib.
57. Cape Breton Island and mainland Nova Scotia.
58. 104.
59. Pierre Berton.
60. Charlottetown, P.E.I.

---

46. The Toughest Questions

1. Monday.
2. It was the cover used for women employed at Camp X, the secret training camp near Pickering, Ont. Ian Fleming trained there as well.
3. Joan Miller, born in Nelson, B.C., was the first person to appear on the world's first television program. The program, "Picture Page," inaugurated BBC's television service, the first in the world, on 2 Nov. 1936.
4. Michal Bryan. Bernard Mara.
5. "Thank you." He said this to his nurse.
6. The so-called Symphony Six were six regular members of the Toronto Symphony Orchestra who were refused entry when the orchestra was invited to perform in the United States in 1951. This was during the

McCarthy-inspired "witch hunt." Matters worsened when the orchestra failed to renew their contracts the following year. The six musicians were: Dick Keetbass, William Kuinka, Abe Mannheim, John Moskalyk, Ruth Ross, and Steven Staryk.

7. Joan O'Malley sewed the first Maple Leaf flag in 1964.
8. Bungee, a mixture of Scots, Cree, French, etc.
9. The Japanese explorer trekked for fifty-four days across the frozen Arctic Ocean until he reached the North Pole. He did this alone by dogsled.
10. A. Phimister Proctor.
11 "Hoy, hoy!"
12. Peter Allen succeeded Milton Cross on 4 Jan. 1975.
13. Canada Bay is located on the east coast of Newfoundland.

---

47. Geography in General

1. Northern Hemisphere.
2. North America.
3. Quebec is the largest province, Prince Edward Island the smallest.
4. Prince Edward Island, although the smallest island with the smallest population, has the highest average density — 51 persons per square mile.
5. Franklin, Keewatin, and Mackenzie.
6. Newfoundland, Nova Scotia, and Prince Edward Island.
7. The four points are geographical extremes of Canada.
   A. Middle Island is the southernmost point.
   B. Cape Columbia is the northernmost point.
   C. Cape Spear is the easternmost point.
   D. Mount St. Elias is the westernmost point.
8. Center.
9. True.
10. Alaska. Juneau. Yukon Territory.
11. St. Pierre and Miquelon. France. b. 93 square miles. Langlade is the third and smallest island of the group.
12. Greenland. Denmark.
13. Siberia. Soviet Union or U.S.S.R.

---

48. Water Everywhere

1. False. Canada has the most fresh water of any country, including the Soviet Union.
2. False. The Mackenzie River is the country's longest.
3. True.
4. B.
5. Quebec.
6. False. In fact, the reverse is true: Ontario has ten times the fresh water British Columbia has.
7. British Columbia.
8. Lake Superior.
9. The Rideau River.
10. A. Lake Superior and Lakes Michigan and Huron.
    B. Lake Erie and Lake Ontario.
11. Georgian Bay.
12. Lake Manitou is Canada's only dead sea. Its salt content is so high, nothing lives in it. Thus it resembles Salt Lake City in Utah, and the Dead Sea in Israel.
13. The Bay of Fundy separates New Brunswick and Nova Scotia.
14. American Falls and Canadian (or Horseshoe) Falls.
15. "businessman."

---

49. What Province is This?

1. Yukon.
2. Saskatchewan.
3. Prince Edward Island.
4. Nova Scotia.
5. Quebec.
6. Alberta.
7. New Brunswick.
8. Ontario.
9. Newfoundland.
10. Manitoba.
11. British Columbia.
12. Northwest Territories.

---

50. On Mountains

1. Shining.
2. True.
3. B. Everest is 8,848 metres (29,028 feet) high, or 2,798 metres (9,178 feet) higher than Mount Logan.
4. Rocky Mountains.

5. Torngat Mountains, Nfld.
6. Laurentian Mountains.
7. A. Mount Bumpus, Victoria Range, N.W.T.
   C. Eiffel Peak, Alta.
8. *Valley.*

10. B.
11. Your Highness. Ma'am.

---

51. Islands Ahoy

1. A.
2. False. Labrador (112,826 sq. mi.) is approximately three times the size of the island of Newfoundland (43,359 sq. mi.).
3. Vancouver Island.
4. Southampton Island.
5. Baffin Island.
6. Freshwater.
7. Newfoundland (143,045 sq. mi.) is larger than Vancouver Island (12,408 sq. mi.).
8. Baffin Island is bigger than both the island of Newfoundland and Labrador.
9. True.
10. Newfoundland was colonized by the Vikings about 1,000 A.D.
11. Prince Edward Island is so covered by the *Charlettown Guardian.*
12. Newfoundland.

---

52. The Monarchy

1. F. i.
   A. ii.
   D. iii.
   B. iv.
   E. v.
   C. vi.
2. Louis the Fifteenth, who ruled from 1714 to 1774.
3. George II, who ruled from 1727 to 1760, was on the throne at the fall of New France. He was succeeded the following year by George III, during whose reign the American colonies succeeded in their revolt.
4. Wales. Alberta. Windsor.
5. George. Elizabeth. World War II.
6. Grace of God. The Commonwealth. Faith.
7. Mountbatten. Edinburgh. Consort. Anne. Edward.
8. Wales. Boss.
9. The Queen. A Governor General.

53. Who Was the P.M. Then?

1. Lester B. Pearson.
2. W.L. Mackenzie King.
3. W.L. Mackenzie King.
4. Sir Wilfrid Laurier.
5. Louis St. Laurent.
6. Sir Robert Borden (leading the Union Government).
7. Sir John A. Macdonald.
8. Sir Wilfrid Laurier.
9. Governor General Roland Michener.

---

54. Prime Ministers

1. Sir John A. Macdonald.
2. Alexander Mackenzie.
7. Sir Charles Tupper.
8. Sir Wilfrid Laurier.
12. Arthur Meighen.
14. R.B. Bennett.
15. W.L. Mackenzie King.
17. John G. Diefenbaker.
20. Joe Clark.
21. Pierre Elliott Trudeau.

---

55. Who's Who: Prime Ministers

1: K.		9.	I.
2. F.		10.	B.
3. N.		11.	O.
4. D.		12.	H.
5. M.		13.	C.
6. A.		14.	L.
7. E.		15.	J.
8. G.		16.	P.

---

56. Who's Who: Governors General

1. Lord Dufferin, 1872-78.
2. Lord Stanley, 1888-93.
3. Lord Grey, 1904-11.
4. Lord Byng, 1921-26.
5. Lord Bessborough, 1931-35.
6. John Buchan, Lord Tweedsmuir, 1935-40.
7. Vincent Massey, 1952-59.

8. Major-General Georges-Philias Vanier, 1959-67. (Credit: Cavouk Portraits)

9. D. Roland Michener, 1967-74. (Credit: Cavouk Portraits)

10. Jules Léger, 1974-79. (Credit: M. Bedford)

11. Edward Schreyer, 1979- . (Credit: Cavouk Portraits)

(Unless otherwise indicated, photos courtesy Public Archives Canada)

57. Royal Commissions

1. B.	7. B.
2. C.	8. A.
3. A.	9. C.
4. A.	10. A.
5. B.	11. C.
6. C.	

58. Fields of Honor

1. B.

2. C. (Nobody 'won,' but the Americans did withdraw.)

3. A.

4. B. (There were, however, 5,700 casualties.)

5. A.

6. C.

59. Momentous Dates

1. The Hudson's Bay Company is chartered.

2. Conquest of Quebec by the British at the Plains of Abraham.

3. The British North America Act effects a union of British colonies.

4. Louis Riel is hanged for treason, Regina.

5. Gold is discovered on Bonanza Creek, Klondike River, Yukon.

6. The Canadian Corps takes Vimy Ridge, France.

7. Signing of the armistice ends First World War.

8. Winnipeg General Strike is called.

9. Canada declares war on Germany.

10. October Crisis commences with kidnapping of James Cross, Montreal.

60. Historic Quotations

1. Major-General James Wolfe, after reciting Gray's "Elegy," prior to the Battle of the Plains of Abraham, 13 Sept. 1759.

2. Sir Alexander Mackenzie, the first person to cross the country from east to west on foot, left this "brief memorial" on a rock on the shore of Dean Channel, Bella Coola River, B.C., 1793.

3. Sir Isaac Brock's dying command, or believed to be so, at the Battle of Queenston Heights in the War of 1812, 13 Oct. 1812.

4. Lord Durham, in his famous *Report* (1839), on the French and the English.

5. George Stephen, president of the CPR, exhorting Donald Smith in Scotland to promote the railway's interests by invoking the might of the rock near their birthplace in northern Scotland, 1884.

6. Louis Riel, Métis leader, in his defense speech during his trial for treason, Regina, 31 July 1885.

7. W.L. Mackenzie King, prime minister, on the need of conscription during World War II.

8. Lester B. Pearson, Nobel Prize acceptance speech, Oslo, 11 Dec. 1957.

9. Charles de Gaulle, President of the French Republic, voicing the separatist slogan from the balcony of the Montreal City Hall, 24 July 1967.

10. Paul Henderson, hockey player, after scoring the final goal in the Team Canada-Russia hockey series in Moscow, 28 Sept. 1972.

11. René Lévesque, leader of the Parti Québècois, the evening of his party's electoral victory, 15 Nov. 1976.

12. Ken Taylor, Canadian Ambassador to Iran, after organizing the so-called Canadian caper — offering sanctuary and then the means of escape to six American citizens caught in revolutionary Teheran, Jan. 1980.

61. Explorers and Discoverers

Part One	Part Two
1. F.	7. D.
2. E.	8. E.
3. D.	9. G.
4. A.	10. A.
5. C.	11. F.
6. B.	12. B.
	13. C.

62. Disastrous Dates

1. Great Quebec Earthquake.
2. The Frank Slide, Alta.
3. *Empress of Ireland* sinks in the Gulf of St. Lawrence.
4. Fire guts the Centre Block, Parliament Hill, Ottawa.
5. Halifax Explosion.
6. Winnipeg Flood. Flooding lasted from two to four weeks, but was at its height on 19 May.
7. Hurricane Hazel hits Toronto.
8. Springhill Mine Disaster, N.S.

---

63. Least-Liked Men

1. Adrien Arcand (1899-1967), a leading fascist in Montreal, was an effective speaker and writer. He edited a series of newspapers, including *Le Goglu* in 1929, and *Le Patriote* in 1933, and headed a fascist party or two. He was anti-communist and anti-semitic, pro-Catholicism and pro-Quebec. He was interned during the Second World War.

2. François Bigot (1703-78), the last Intendant of New France, was infamous for his financial misdeeds. His corrupt administration of Quebec earned him eleven months in the Bastille and then banishment from his native France.

3. Charles Lawrence (1709-60), as lieutenant-governor of Nova Scotia, personally ordered the deportation of the Acadians in 1755. For this single act he earned the undying enmity of these French-speaking people and their many supporters.

4. Robert Stobo (1726-70), a Scots-born Virginian, took credit for convincing General Wolfe to attack Quebec in 1759 by way of Anse au Foulon, now known as Wolfe's Cove. Earlier that year he had escaped from imprisonment in Quebec. He is no hero to the French in Canada.

5. Louis-Joseph Papineau (1786-1871) was the rebel leader in the Rebellion of 1837 in Lower Canada, and as such was detested by the non-Patriotes. He fled to the United States before the first major engagement at Saint-Denis and, hence, was despised by many of the Patriotes as well. Much the same feeling was generated by his co-insurrectionist, William Lyon Mackenzie (1795-1861), who led the Rebellion in Upper Canada. In later life, both were rehabilitated.

6. John Strachan (1778-1867), the first Bishop of Toronto, was a pillar of the establishment, the Family Compact. As such the Reformers in Upper Canada despised him in much the same way the Patriotes in Lower Canada detested the leaders of the Château Clique.

7. Lord Durham (1792-1840), governor general of British North America, authored in 1839 his famous *Report* which dismissed the French Canadians as having no history or culture and recommended the introduction of a form of responsible government. Thus he incurred the rancor of French Canadians to this day, and of the governing elite of his day, though history has treated him and his brilliant report better than did his contemporaries.

8. Louis Riel (1844-85), central figure in the Red River Rebellion and the North West Rebellion, was hanged for treason in Regina ("though every dog in Quebec bark in his favour," gloated Sir John A. Macdonald). He divided the country religiously, socially, racially, and politically. He is now seen as the champion of minority rights and the conscience of his people.

9. Sir Joseph Flavelle (1858-1939), financier and philanthropist, was accused of profiteering on foodstuffs sent to the troops overseas during World War I. He protested his innocence but to no avail. In retrospect it seems he may have been engaged in practices that were common at the time or the accusations may even have been based on misinformation.

10. R.B. Bennett (1870-1947), prime minister, led the country during the worst years of the Depression. As a prosperous lawyer and businessman, he acted as a lightning rod for the abuse and vituperation of the unemployed who dubbed horse-drawn automobiles "Bennett buggies." Also despised, though mostly on account of his cold manner, was the earlier prime minister, Arthur Meighen (1874-1960).

11. Fred Rose was the first — and so far only — Communist to sit in the House

of Commons. Evidence that implicated Rose in Soviet espionage activities was uncovered in 1945, when Igor Gouzenko defected from the Russian Embassy in Ottawa. Rose was tried, found guilty, and imprisoned. In 1983 he was alive and well and living in Warsaw, an object of contempt to a great many.

12. Paul Rose was a leading member of the FLQ who kidnapped and then murdered Pierre Laporte at the height of the October Crisis of 1970. He was found guilty of murder and currently languishes in a Quebec prison. There is still sympathy for the FLQ members, if not for such deeds as the "execution" of Laporte.

13. Clifford Olson is the worst mass murderer in Canadian history. In the late 1970s and early 1980s, he brutally murdered at least eleven children and youths in British Columbia. In 1982 the RCMP actually reimbursed him for his detailed confession, thereby bringing contempt down upon the Force as well as upon Olson.

64. Brave Men and Women
1. F. 5. C.
2. E. 6. A.
3. D. 7. B.
4. G.

65. Love Stories
1. Marguerite de La Roque is the name of the unfortunate woman who lost everything short of life itself.

2. Evangeline is the name of this symbolic Acadian heroine whose lover was sent to Louisiana following the expulsion of the Acadians in 1755. The American poet Henry Wadsworth Longfellow based his narrative poem *Evangeline: A Tale of Acadie* (1847) on the story.

3. The Duke of Kent's daughter, born in 1818, ascended the throne as Queen Victoria.

4. The woman's name was Adele Hugo and she was the daughter of the French novelist Victor Hugo. Truffaut's film, a study in obsession, is called *The Story of Adele H.* (1975).

5. The couple, of course, is Margaret Sinclair and Pierre Elliott Trudeau, who were married in 1971 and separated in 1977. Their three children are Michel, Sasha, and Justin.

66. Mottoes and Slogans
1. F. 5. H.
2. E. 6. B.
3. D. 7. C.
4. A. 8. G.

67. Newspapering People
1. G.   9. B.
2. F. 10. C.
3. K. 11. M.
4. A. 12. H.
5. J. 13. O.
6. N. 14. D.
7. L. 15. I.
8. E. 16. P.

68. Bits and Pieces
1. *TV Guide.*
2. Allan Fotheringham.
3. *Halifax.*
4. *L'Actualité.*
5. Sports.
6. False. The paper with the greatest circulation is the *Toronto Star.*
7. It was moved to Montreal because the province of Quebec, unlike Ontario, permitted the publication of liquor advertisements in the 1930s.
8. The *Globe and Mail.*
9. *TV-Hebdo.*
10. A. Allan Fotheringham.
    B. Charles Lynch.
    C. Dalton Camp.
    D. John Fraser.
    E. Peter Newman.
    F. Richard Gwyn.
    G. Geoffrey Stevens.
11. *La Presse.*
12. Nathan Cohen.
13. Edith Josie. She wrote for the *Whitehorse Star* from 1962.
14. Southam.
15. Thomson.
16. Canadian Press. The letters for thirty, set off by dashes, was the signal used by telegraphers that this was the end of the message. It was later used by reporters, editors, and typesetters.

69. Differences in English

1		A.	Flat
2.	Candy.	B.	
3.		C.	Torch.
4.		D.	Pavement.
5.	Kerosens.	E.	
6.		F.	Lodger.
7.		G.	Wing.
8.		H.	Dynamo.
9.	Hood.	I.	
10.	Wrench.	J.	
11.		K.	Silencer.
12.		L.	Lorry.
13.		M.	Trunk road.
14.	Detour.	N.	
15.		O.	Petrol station.

70. Languages: Official and Unofficial

The figures that follow are generalizations based on Population by Mother Tongue (1971 Census).

1. False. Italian-speakers numbered 538,360; Ukrainian-speakers, 309,855.
2. False. Russian is spoken by 31,745; Welsh, 3,160.
3. True. German is the mother tongue of 561,085 Canadians.
4. The Inuit language is called Inuktitut.
5. True. Dutch is spoken by 144,925 Canadians, Polish by 134,780. That's close enough.
6. True. Scottish Canadians number 1,720,390; Irish Canadians number 1,581,730.
7. True. The figures are: English, 12,973,810; French, 5,793,650.

71. Historic Acts

1.	G.	7.	C.
2.	E.	8.	F.
3.	H.	9.	B.
4.	L.	10.	D.
5.	A.	11.	I.
6.	K.	12.	J.

72. Criminals

1.	H.	7.	B.
2.	K.	8.	E.
3.	I.	9.	D.
4.	L.	10.	J.
5.	G.	11.	C.
6.	A.	12.	F.

73. Identify That Verse

1. Lines from "Indian Summer" by William Wilfred Campbell.
2. Lines from "The Song My Paddle Sings" by E. Pauline Johnson.
3. Lines from "In Flanders Fields" by John McCrae.
4. Lines from "The Shooting of Dan McGrew" by Robert W. Service.
5. Lines from "Laurentian Shield" by F.R. Scott.
6. Lines from "The Lonely Land" by A.J.M. Smith.
7. Lines from "David" by Earle Birney.
8. Lines from "The Birth of Tragedy" by Irving Layton.

74. Top Ten Novels

1. *The Stone Angel* by Margaret Laurence.
2. *Fifth Business* by Robertson Davies.
3. *As For Me and My House* by Sinclair Ross.
4. *The Mountain and the Valley* by Ernest Buckler.
5. *The Tin Flute* by Gabrielle Roy.
6. *The Apprenticeship of Duddy Kravitz* by Mordecai Richler.
7. *The Double Hook* by Sheila Watson.
8. *The Watch that Ends the Night* by Hugh MacLennan.
9. *Who Has Seen the Wind* by W.O. Mitchell.
10. *The Diviners* by Margaret Laurence.

75. Novel Beginnings

1.	F.	7.	A.
2.	H.	8.	B.
3.	I.	9.	L.
4.	E.	10.	J.
5.	C.	11.	G.
6.	K.	12.	D.

76. Pen Names

1.	H.	6.	E.
2.	D.	7.	G.
3.	C.	8.	B.
4.	I.	9.	F.
5.	A.		

77. Biographies and Autobiographies

1. H. (By Peter C. Newman)

2. J. (By Peter C. Newman)
3. F. (By Joseph Schull)
4. C. (or K.) (By Smallwood)
5. G. (By Bruce Hutchison)
6. B. (By William Stevenson)
7. A. (By Richard Gwyn)
8. D. (By Donald Creighton)
9. E. (By Peter C. Newman)
10. I. (By Gouzenko)
11. K. (or C.) (By Richard Gwyn)

78. Pot-Pourri

1. Bertram Brooker.
2. *Turvey* is the title of the first and third editions; the second, unauthorized edition was called *The Kootenay Highlander*.
3. *The Incomparable Atuk.*
4. Leacock Medal for Humour.
5. False. *Songs of a Sourdough* is the title of the first, Canadian edition; *The Spell of the Yukon* is the title of the second, American edition.
6. Morley Callaghan.
7. Paul Hébert.
8. Emile Nelligan.
9. *Mountain Meadow. Sick Heart River.*
10. Hugh MacLennan.
11. *In High Places.*
12. Charles Cochrane is the author of *Christianity and Classical Culture.*
13. T. Lobsang Rampa. *The Third Eye.*
14. The New Age.
15. A. Brooke wrote the first novel set in what is now Canada. It was published in London, England.
    B. Hart wrote the first novel set in and published in what is now Canada. It was issued by subscription in Kingston, U.C. (Ont.).
16. The novel is *Cabbagetown* and the author is Hugh Garner.
17. *I Heard the Owl Call My Name* was written by Margaret Craven.

79. Literary Locales

1. I. Avonlea is the fictitious setting of *Anne of Green Gables* and its seven sequels. L.M. Montgomery modeled the community on Cavendish on the north shore of Prince Edward Island.
2. H. Crocus resembles Weyburn, Sask., and High River, Alta., towns

associated with W.O. Mitchell who created the fictitious southern Saskatchewan setting for the CBC Radio and Television series and stories of *Jake and the Kid.*
3. G. Fletcher's Field is the name for Baron Byng High School on St. Urbain Street in Montreal, chosen by Mordecai Richler for *The Apprenticeship of Duddy Kravitz* and *St. Urbain's Horseman.*
4. E. The fictitious city of Grantham resembles St. Catharines, Ont., the stamping ground of Benny Cooperman, private-eye hero of Howard Engel's *The Suicide Murders*, etc.
5. C. Mazo de la Roche modeled the ancestral home of the Whiteoaks on "Benares," a country home built at Clarkson, Ont., and called it Jalna in the novel of that name and its fourteen sequels.
6. J. The fictional town of Manawaka, located some hundred miles north of Winnipeg by Margaret Laurence in such novels as *The Stone Angel*, may be a contraction of MANitoba and her birthplace of NeepAWA.
7. A. An isolated community in the B.C. interior, Namko is the setting of the CBC-TV series *Cariboo Country*, written by Paul St. Pierre and based on his novel *Breaking Smith's Quarter Horse* (1966).
8. B. Péribonca is the name of an actual community in the Lac Saint-Jean region of Quebec; imaginatively it is also the locale of the Habitants described so lovingly by Louis Hémon in *Maria Chapdelaine.*
9. F. Gabrielle Roy lived on Rue Deschambault in St. Boniface, Man.; *Rue Deschambault* is the original title of the novel known in English as *Street of Riches.*
10. D. Salterton is loosely based on Kingston, Ont., by Robertson Davies in *Tempest Tost, Leaven of Malice*, and *A Mixture of Frailties.*

80. Metric Commission

1. Length. (Foot)
2. Speed. (Miles per hour)
3. Area. (Acres)
4. Volume. (Gallon)
5. Mass. (Pound)

6. Temperature. (Degree Fahrenheit)
7. Time. (Minute)
8. Power. (Kilowatt)
9. Pressure. (Pound)

81. Metric Equivalents

1. 16.09. 4. 25.4.
2. 4.50.   5. .568.
3. 33.3°. 6. 4.55.

82. Metric Expressions

1. I love you, a bushel and a peck.
2. A spoonful of sugar makes the medicine go down.
3. A graveyard is God's acre.
4. How many miles to Babylon?
5. Spare the rod and spoil the child. (This is a pun on the word "rod" which has the double meaning of a switch and a land measure [of 5.5 yards].)
6. It came down like a ton of bricks. ("Tonne" is SI, "ton" is Imperial.)
7. A miss is as good as a mile.
8. There was a crooked man, and he walked a crooked mile.
9. Give him an inch and he'll take a mile.
10. Every inch a king. (The metric version reads better, loosely "translated" as "Every millimetre a monarch.")
11. I'd walk a mile for a Camel.
12. An ounce of prevention is worth a pound of cure.

83. Alphametric Puzzle

I am grateful to Elisabeth Hallamore, author of *The Metric Book* (1974), for the following values:

A — 0   G — 5
M — 1   L — 6
S — 2   T — 7
E — 3   C — 8
R — 4   I — 9

84. Academy Canadiana

1. T.   8. B.   15. O.
2. G or H.   9. S.   16. L.
3. Q.   10. C.   17. E.
4. N.   11. D.   18. F.
5. J.   12. R.   19. I.
6. P.   13. K.   20. M.
7. A.   14. H. or G.

85. Stars Across Canada

1. *The 49th Parallel* (1941).
2. *Niagara* (1952).
3. *Russian Roulette* (1975).
4. *The 13th Letter* (1951).
5. *Rose Marie* (1954).
6. *I Confess* (1953).

86. Real History

1. E.   4. I.   7. C.
2. H.   5. B.   8. F.
3. A.   6. D.   9. G.

87. Great Documentary Films

1. *Universe* (NFB, 1960). The narrator is Douglas Rain, the producer Tom Daly.
2. *City of Gold* (NFB, 1957), written and narrated by Pierre Berton, is about Dawson City and the Gold Rush.
3. *Nanook of the North* (Pathé, 1922) was conceived and directed by Robert Flaherty. Filming took place at Inoucdjouac, Northern Ungava, Que. The sponsor was Revillon Frères, now part of the Hudson's Bay Company.
4. *Warrendale* (King, 1966), produced by Patrick Watson and directed by Allan King. It was filmed at Warrendale, a Toronto-area treatment center for disturbed children.
5. *Neighbours* (NFB, 1952), a film by Norman McLaren. It photographed live action in the manner of animation. It was awarded the 1952 Documentary — Short Subject Oscar.
6. Bonus answer: the NFB produced all but two of the above documentaries; *Nanook of the North* and *Warrendale* were privately produced.

88. Songs That Were Dear

1. B.   6. A.   11. C.
2. A.   7. C.   12. A.
3. C.   8. C.   13. A.
4. A.   9. B.   14. C.
5. C.   10. A.   15. C.

89. Hit Songs

1. A.   7. A.   13. B.
2. A.   8. A.   14. A.
3. B.   9. A.   15. A.
4. A.   10. B.   16. A.
5. A.   11. B.   17. B.
6. A.   12. A.   18. B.

90. Musical Groups

1. G.	7. M.	13. J.
2. F.	8. E.	14. R.
3. L.	9. O.	15. A.
4. N.	10. B.	16. Q.
5. H.	11. P.	17. K.
6. D.	12. C.	18. I.

91. Original Operas

1. B.	6. E.
2. H.	7. D.
3. I.	8. G.
4. C.	9. A.
5. F.	

92. Original Ballets

1. C.	5. C.
2. B.	6. A.
3. C.	7. C.
4. B.	

93. Musical Medley

1. Yes.
2. Yes.
3. No. Quilico is a baritone, but Vickers is a tenor.
4. Yes.
5. No. They were permanent conductors of the Toronto Symphony.
6. No. Hank Snow is known as Hank, and Ameen Ganam is known as King Ganam. Wilf Carter is identified with the sobriquets "Montana Slim" and "The Yodelling Cowboy."
7. No. Hibbs comes from Bell Island, Nfld.
8. Yes.
9. Yes.
10. No. They were popular but they were not dance bands, being country bands.
11. No. The ensemble is a quintet, with one more member, William Phillips, later replaced by Fred Mills.
12. No. Adaskin directed *Opportunity Knocks*; Battle, *Singing Stars of Tomorrow*.
13. No. Both are leading jazz performers, Peterson as a pianist, Davidson as a cornetist.
14. Yes.
15. Yes.
16. Yes.
17. Yes.
18. Yes.

94. Anthems

1. "O Canada." "God Save the Queen."
2. Words. Music. Weir.
3. Alfred, Lord Tennyson.
4. The skies. The line runs "Beneath thy shining skies/May stalwart song and gentle maidens rise."
5. "The Maple Leaf Forever." Muir.
6. "Alouette." The Rebellion of 1837. "_____ Pays." Gilles Vigneault wrote "Mon Pays" (My Country).
7. Roger Doucet.
8. "CA-NA-DA." Scouts.
9. "_____ Salute."

95. Three of a Kind

1. Claire.	19. Sandfield.
2. Wilfred.	20. D'Arcy.
3. Etienne.	21. Lyon.
4. Valancy.	22. Maud.
5. Ward.	23. Wilson.
6. Henry.	24. McCall.
7. Jeanette.	25. Joseph.
8. Lou.	26. Guy.
9. Louis.	27. Luc.
10. Kenneth.	28. Guy.
11. Geiger.	29. Esprit.
12. Irving.	30. Collingwood.
13. Philip.	31. Louis.
14. Jean.	32. Goodman.
15. Blok.	33. Anne.
16. Brownell.	34. Campbell.
17. Jones.	35. Parr.
18. Kirkland.	

96. Great Canadians

1. Sir Frederick Banting.
2. Alexander Graham Bell.
3. Joseph Elzéar Bernier.
4. Henri Bourassa.
5. Emily Carr.
6. Sir Thomas Chapais.
7. Sir Arthur Currie.
8. C.H. "Punch" Dickins.
9. Timothy Eaton.
10. Sir Sandford Fleming.
11. Gratien Gélinas.
12. Alain Grandbois.
13. George Monro Grant.
14. Harold Adams Innis.
15. Stephen Leacock.
16. Paul-Emile Cardinal Léger.
17. Sir William Osler.

18. E.J. Pratt.
19. Gabrielle Roy.
20. Sir Charles E. Saunders.
21. Lord Strathcona.
22. Tom Thomson.
23. J.B. Tyrrell.
24. Sir William Cornelius Van Horne.
25. J.S. Woodsworth.

97. Public Figures

1. F.	6. I.	11. M.	16. N.
2. E.	7. A.	12. L.	17. P.
3. C.	8. G.	13. Q.	18. R.
4. H.	9. S.	14. O.	19. T.
5. B.	10. D.	15. K.	20. J.

98. All Sorts

1. Herman.
2. Eddy, the founder of the E.B. Eddy Co. Ltd., was known as "the greatest matchmaker in the world." Bennett for a time held controlling interest in the match company.
3. The names are aliases assumed by Ferdinand Waldo Demara, the so-called Great Imposter, while he practiced his deceptions in Canada.
4. Sir William Stephenson, inventor, financier, and World War II security head.
5. Johnson is the "Trapper," Morrison the "Outlaw."
6. Elizabeth Arden, who was born Florence Nightingale Graham in Woodbridge, Ont.
7. Bob Hope.
8. "Radishes and Gooseberries."
9. The right was the custom that Anglican bishops take their titles from their sees — Fleming's from the Arctic, Strachan from Toronto.
10. "Margery the Medium." She was also called "The Blonde Witch of Boston."
11. Alvin (Creepy) Karpis.
12. Xaviera Hollander.
13. These names are aliases assumed while on the run in Toronto by James Earl Ray, assassin of Martin Luther King.
14. Mrs. Bigley operated under a number of aliases as a swindler. She had a penchant for jewellery — other people's.

99. Native Writers

1. E. Pauline Johnson.
2. Chief Dan George.
3. Markoosie.
4. George C. Clutesi.
5. Pitseolak.
6. Maria Campbell.

100. Indian Languages

```
                              H   I
        K O L U S C H A       A   N
          A   S       A I     I   U
          L   I K T   T T     D   K
          G   O O S   H A     A   T
      I R O Q U O T I H A P   N   I
         N   A U T M P       N   T
          K   N E S A S           U
          I   N H I C             T
          A   A A I A
          N   Y A A N
      W A K A S H A N
    S A L I S H A N
```

101. How Good Is Your Indian?

1. A caribou is a type of deer.
2. A chipmunk is a squirrel; it derives its name from the Algonkian for "headfirst," for it descends the trunks of trees head down.
3. Manitou is the word for "spirit" or "mystery."
4. A moccasin is a leather shoe or slipper.
5. The moose is the largest member of the deer family.
6. Muskeg is Algonkian for "swamp."
7. A papoose is Algonkian for a baby or young child.
8. Pemmican is preserved buffalo or caribou meat, a staple of the fur trade and the Plains Indians of the past.
9. A pow-wow is a meeting for ceremonial or official purposes.
10. A skunk is a white-striped, bushy-tailed animal able to emit a powerful stench.
11. A toboggan is a long sleigh.
12. A tomahawk is a war-axe.
13. A totem is an object or image of emblematic significance.
14. A wapiti is an elk.
15. Wigwam is the Algonkian word for a conical hut; the word teepee is of Dakotan origin used in the West.

102. Indian Leaders

1. D.   4. B.
2. C.   5. E.
3. A.   6. F.

103. First Indians

1. Calder. British Columbia.
2. Gladstone. The Senate.
3. Marchand. House of Commons. British Columbia.
4. Steinhauer. Alberta. lieutenant-governor. Alberta.

104. How Good Is Your Inuktitut?

1. House. Snow.
2. The people.
3. *Kamiks* (Eastern Arctic) or *mukluks* (Western Arctic).
4. *Kayak. Umiak.*
5. Dog.
6. *Tornit.* (*Toronto* and *nit.*)
7. White man, stranger.
8. A *shaman* is a medicine man, priest, wizard, or prophet. A *parka* is a hooded jacket made of fur.
9. Snow.

105. Eskimo Ethos

1. An *inukshuk* is a human-like form built of stone blocks by Eskimos to serve as a landmark. In Inuktitut it means "in lieu of a man."
2. B.
3. Eskimo Brotherhood.
4. Wrong. *Agaguk* is the title of Yves Thériault's novel about an Eskimo hunter of the same name. Flaherty's film is called *Nanook of the North* and is about a hunter and harpooner.
5. Soapstone.
6. The Igloo Tag.
7. The Methodist was James Evans, the Anglican E.J. Peck. The system of writing was shorthand, shapes which Evans used in his Cree Syllabic.
8. A.
9. James Houston.
10. Northwest Territories.
11. *Enchanted.* Kenojuak. Centennial.
12. Nanook is the name of the Belcher Island Eskimo who starred in *Nanook of the North*, Robert J. Flaherty's documentary film which, as the director noted, was seen in places where viewers had to be told that the white on the screen was snow.

106. Political Catch-Phrases

1. "_____ Government."
2. "_____ Nations."
3. "_____ Pop." (That is, Representation by Population.)
4. "_____ First."
5. "_____ Policy."
6. "_____ the Talents." (Also known as "the Ministry of All Talents.")
7. "_____ Canada."
8. "_____ Ottawa."
9. "_____ Chaos."
10. "Northern _____."
11. "_____ to Lose?"
12. "*Maîtres* _____."
13. "Quiet _____."
14. "One _____."
15. "_____ Resources."
16. "_____ Decision."
17. "Co-operative _____."
18. "_____ Just _____."
19. "_____ Machine."
20. "Action _____."
21. "_____ Strong."
22. "_____ Bums."
23. "Sovereignty _____."
24. "_____ Communities."
25. "_____ socialist hoards _____." Bennett used the phrase for twenty years.

107. Constituencies

1. F.   7. E.
2. K.   8. D.
3. I.   9. C.
4. H.   10. J.
5. B.   11. A.
6. G.

108. Floral Emblems

1. H.   7. F.
2. K.   8. E.
3. J.   9. B.
4. I.   10. D.
5. C.   11. G.
6. A.   12. L.

109. Populations

1. L.	7. J.
2. K.	8. C.
3. H.	9. A.
4. E.	10. B.
5. D.	11. I.
6. F.	12. G.

110. Premiers Since Confederation

1. H.	7. B. (or K.)
2. I.	8. F.
3. J.	9. K. (or B.)
4. E.	10. G.
5. D.	11. C.
6. A.	

The mystery province is: (K) Nova Scotia.

111. Names on Maps

1. Sir Isaac Brock is remembered in the name of Brockville, Ont., and the monument in his honor was erected at Queenston Heights, Ont.
2. Bligh Island, B.C., was named after Captain Bligh.
3. Cavendish, N.S., was named after Henry Cavendish (1731-1810).
4. Carcross, Y.T.
5. Dickens. Dickens. Dickens. Dickens. Dickens.
6. Estevan, Sask., derives acronymically from Georg*E* *ST*Ephen and William Cornelius *VAN* Horne.
7. Ingonish, N.S.
8. Lachine, Que.
9. Second World War. The lakes commemorate those Canadians who died in these engagements.
10. Ottawa (changed in 1855 from Bytown).
11. Poe, Alta., was named after Edgar Allan Poe (1809-1849).
12. Charles Kingsley is the novelist. Sir Thomas More is the other author.
13. Taber, Alta.
14. Moose Jaw, Sask.

112. New Place Names

1. Manitoba
2. Kitchener outpolled the four other names (followed by Brock, Adanac, Corona, then Benton). The town was formerly called Berlin.
3. Ile Royale became Cape Breton. Ile Saint-Jean became Prince Edward Island.
4. Stadacona, Quebec City. Hochelaga, Montreal.
5. Port Arthur and Fort William amalgamated into Thunder Bay.
6. A. Wascana means Pile of Bones. B. Regina.
7. B.
8. Toronto.

113. Scrambled Place Names

Part One	Part Two
1. Bella Coola.	1. Gander. (Nfld.)
2. Regina.	2. Petit Nord. (P.E.I.)
3. Kelowna.	3. Tracadie. (P.E.I.)
4. Edmonton.	4. Canso. (N.S.)
5. Squamish.	5. Fogo Island. (Nfld.)
6. Winnipeg.	6. Montreal. (Que.)
7. Kamloops.	7. Carbonear. (Nfld.)
8. Saskatoon.	8. Toronto. (Ont.)
9. Nelson.	9. Rothesay. (N.B.)

114. Famous Sights

1. Peggy's Cove, Halifax County, Nova Scotia. (Nova Scotia Department Government Services)
2. Lake Louise, Alberta. (Travel Alberta)
3. Memorial University, St. John's, Newfoundland. (Nfld. Tourist Services Division)
4. Lions Gate Bridge, Vancouver, British Columbia. (Tourism B.C.)
5. Magnetic Hill, Moncton, New Brunswick. (New Brunswick Department of Tourism)
6. Green Gables, Cavendish, Prince Edward Island. (P.E.I. Tourism)
7. Pont Pierre-Laporte, Quebec City. (Gouvernement du Québec)
8. Butchart Gardens, Victoria, British Columbia. (Tourism B.C.)
9. International Peace Gardens, Manitoba - North Dakota border. (Travel Manitoba)
10. Pysanka (Ukrainian Easter Egg), Vegreville, Alberta. (Travel Alberta)
11. Viking Statue, Gimli, Manitoba. (Travel Manitoba)
12. Big Nickel, Sudbury, Ontario. (Ontario Ministry of Industry and Tourism)
13. Louis Riel Statue, Wascana Park, Regina, Saskatchewan. (Saskatchewan Government Photograph)

115. States and Provinces

1. True.
2. False.
3. True.
4. True.
5. False.
6. False.
7. False.
8. False.

116. Holiday Fun in Eastern Canada

1. Louisbourg.
2. Wawa.
3. Bracebridge.
4. Montreal.
5. Point Pelée.
6. Halifax.
7. Quebec City.
8. Percé.
9. Cabot. John Cabot.
10. Hartland.
11. Dryden.

117. Holiday Fun in Western Canada

1. Lethbridge.
2. Vancouver.
3. Vegreville.
4. Calgary.
5. Whitehorse.
6. Banff National Park.
7. Badlands.
8. Barkerville.
9. Hazelton.
10. Winnipeg. (The replica is housed in the Manitoba Museum of Man and Nature.)
11. Regina.

118. National Parks

1. B.
2. A.
3. B.
4. B.
5. B.
6. B.
7. A.
8. B.
9. B.
10. A.
11. A.
12. B.

119. Provincial Parks

1. Newfoundland.
2. Quebec.
3. Manitoba.
4. Prince Edward Island.
5. Ontario.
6. British Columbia.
7. Nova Scotia.
8. Saskatchewan.
9. Alberta.
10. New Brunswick.

120. Notable Regions

1. Cypress Hills, Sask. and Alta.
2. Eastern Townships, Quebec.
3. Okanagan Valley, B.C.
4. Muskoka, Ont.
5. Miramichi Valley, N.B.
6. Ottawa Valley, Ont.
7. Caribou Country, B.C.
8. Annapolis Valley, N.S.
9. Thousand Islands, Ont.

121. Who Said That?

1. Pierre Elliott Trudeau, prime minister, on Canadian-American relations, 1969.
2. David A. Croll, resigning from the Ontario cabinet during the Oshawa strike, 1937.
3. Jay Silverheels, as Tonto, in numerous Lone Ranger movies. The words *Kemo Sabe* are said to mean "Faithful Friend."
4. C.D. Howe, Liberal cabinet minister, attributed in 1945.
5. Jean Drapeau, Montreal mayor, 1975.
6. Raoul Dandurand on Canadian isolationism, at the League of Nations, 1924.
7. Roy Thomson, later Lord Thomson of Fleet, 1957.
8. Pierre Elliott Trudeau, prime minister, 1971.

122. Mystery Quotations

1. FROM SEA TO SEA (Canada's motto, based on Psalm 72:8)
2. THE TRUE NORTH STRONG AND FREE (From the National Anthem)
3. ALL I CAN SAY IS THAT THE WORK HAS BEEN DONE WELL IN EVERY WAY (Sir William C. Van Horne on the completion of the CPR)
4. JE ME SOUVIENS (Quebec's motto, attributed to Eugène Taché)
5. VIVE LE QUEBEC LIBRE! (Charles de Gaulle's declaration)
6. THEY ALWAYS GET THEIR MAN (Unofficial RCMP motto)
7. HE SHOOTS HE SCORES (Foster Hewitt's famous hockey quotation)
8. THE MEDIUM IS THE MESSAGE (Marshall McLuhan's aphorism)
9. LUCK IS BETTER THAN LONG LEGS (Eskimo proverb)

10. MARATHON OF HOPE (Terry Fox's motto)

123. Broadcasting
1. Montreal. CFCF.
2. Canadian Radio Broadcasting Commission.
3. "The Romance of Canada." Montreal. Hudson. Denison. Guthrie.
4. Halifax. J. Frank Willis.
5. True.
6. Rogers Batteryless. CFRB was the first batteryless station in the world.
7. Foster Hewitt.
8. Canadian Radio League. Plaunt. Spry.
9. Trans-Canada. Dominion. Radio.
10. Radio Canada International.
11. The network broadcasts only news. It is known as the CKO All-News network.
12. C.B., or Citizen's Band.

124. Anyone Listening?
1. Wayne is somewhat shorter than Shuster.
2. Woodhouse and Hawkins.
3. Kate Aitken, consumer broadcaster.
4. "CBC Stage," also known as the "Stage Series."
5. Maggie Muggins, for the "Just Mary" show.
6. Max Ferguson.
7. They all said, "Here is the CBC News." In other words, they delivered the national radio news.
8. "Citizens' Forum" and "National Farm Radio Forum."
9. "Court of Opinion."
10. "Assignment."
11. Barbara Frum. Al Maitland.
12. The CBC morning show, now called "Morningside."
13. La Société Radio-Canada.
14. John Fisher.

125. Quiz Programs
1. Roy Ward Dickson.
2. "Trail."
3. "Share the Wealth."
4. "Hamish." Ron Hambleton. Ralph Allen, James Bannerman, and Morley Callaghan.

5. "Fighting Words." Nathan Cohen. "Unrehearsed."

126. Saintly Men and Women
1. E   5. B.
2. C.   6. D.
3. F.   7. G.
4. A.

127. Patron Saints
1. Scotland.
2. David.
3. England.
4. Patrick.
5. France.
6. St. John the Baptist. June.
7. "_____ voice _____ crying _____ wilderness." Cabot. La Société Saint-Jean-Baptiste.

128. Religious Questions
1. Manitou means "spirit" or "mystery."
2. Hutterites.
3. They are associated with Jean de Brébeuf, Jesuit missionary at Huronia, and come from the English version of the Huron Christmas Carol he composed in 1641.
4. Clergy Reserves were Crown lands set aside under the Constitution Act of 1791 in Upper and Lower Canada "for the support and maintenance of the Protestant clergy," which was interpreted by some as meaning that the revenue from the sale of these tracts would support the Church of England. The reserves were a contentious issue until they were secularized in 1854.
5. Maria Monk was an American woman who claimed she had "escaped" from the Hôtel-Dieu, a Catholic convent in Montreal, whose memoirs, The Awful Disclosures of Maria Monk, as Exhibited in a Narrative of Her Sufferings During a Residence of Five Years at the Hôtel-Dieu Nunnery at Montreal, published in 1836, was really the work of an anti-Catholic Presbyterian minister named George Bourne.
6. British-Israel World Federation, or "British Israelites."
7. Evans's gift was the invention of Cree Syllabic, an alphabet for the Cree

nation. He printed some Scriptures in the alphabet of his devising, casting his own type and printing the letters on birchbark. The syllabic system was found so useful, it was adapted by another missionary for use among the Eskimos.

8. Marquis of Lorne, Governor General of Canada (1878-83).

9. Mennonites.

10. Louis Riel.

11. Doukhobors.

12. *Cosmic Consciousness*, published in 1901.

13. The United Church of Canada.

14. E.J. Pratt wrote these lines about Jean de Brébeuf in his narrative poem *Brébeuf and His Brethren*.

15. "Anglican."

16. Igloo.

17. The Church of England in Canada.

18. "Agnosticism."

19. *The Comfortable Pew*.

20. William Kurelek.

21. St. Joseph's Oratory is 125.5 metres (412 feet) high and atop Mount Royal in Montreal.

22. The three largest religious denominations are, in decreasing size, the Roman Catholic Church, the United Church of Canada, and the Anglican Church of Canada.

23. It was first used about the Yukon, but has since been applied to northern wilderness areas.

129. Natural Resources

1. C.	6. H.
2. E.	7. D.
3. G.	8. F.
4. J.	9. B.
5. A.	10. I.

130. Mineral Production

1. PETROLEUM. SULPHUR.
2. COPPER. ZINC.
3. NICKEL. COPPER.
4. ZINC. LEAD.
5. IRON ORE. FLUORSPAR.
6. COAL. GYPSUM.
7. NICKEL. QUARTZ SULPHUR.
8. SAND & GRAVEL.
9. COPPER. ASBESTOS.

10. POTASH. URANIUM.
11. ZINC. SILVER.
12. LEAD. ASBESTOS.
13. MANGANESE. CHROMIUM. BAUXITE. TIN.

131. Black Gold

1. A.

2. Imperial Oil Limited.

3. High quality crude oil was discovered at Leduc, south of Edmonton, in great quantities. This ushered in Canada's "oil age." The well finally went dry in 1974.

4. 320 km. This is the "200-mile limit." Oil.

5. Petro-Canada.

6. Alberta.

7. The Delta is part of the Northwest Territories.

8. Newfoundland will benefit most, as the Hibernia deposits are off the coast of that province.

9. B.

132. Time On Your Hands

1. Standard Time. Sir Sandford Fleming has been called "The Father of Standard Time."

2. Clocks are set forward one hour in the spring, backwards one hour in the fall. Where observed, Daylight Saving Time is in force from the last Sunday in April until the last Sunday in October.

3. The truth of the line is not that the world will come to an end, but that time is relative to locale or time-zone, and that the Newfoundland Standard Time zone is thirty minutes "ahead" of the adjacent Atlantic Standard Time zone.

4. A. iv.
   B. vi.
   C. v.
   D. vii.
   E. iii.
   F. i.
   G. ii.

5. A. 12:00 noon.
   B. 9:00 A.M.
   C. 8:00 A.M.
   D. 11:00 A.M.
   E. 7:00 A.M.
   F. 12:30 P.M.

6. A. 03:17.
   B. 12:00.
   C. 8:18 A.M.
   D. 13:24.
   E. 24:00.
   F. 1.45 P.M.

Rule of Thumb for Conversions

From 24-hour to 12-hour clock: subtract 12:00 from any figure over 12:00 and add P.M.

From 12-hour to 24-hour clock: add 12:00 to any figure over 1:00 P.M. and drop the P.M.

133. Discoveries and Inventions

1. Z.
2. Y.
3. X.
4. W.
5. V.
6. U.
7. T.
8. S.
9. R.
10. Q.
11. P.
12. O.
13. N.
14. M.
15. L.
16. K.
17. J.
18. I.
19. H.
20. G.
21. F.
22. E.
23. D.
24. C.
25. B.
26. A.

134. Famous Physicians

1. N.
2. P.
3. F.
4. I.
5. M.
6. T.
7. C.
8. H.
9. J.
10. B.
11. Q.
12. E.
13. O.
14. K.
15. R.
16. L.
17. D.
18. A.
19. G.
20. S.

135. Space Age

1. Meteorites.
2. River. Atomic Energy of Canada Ltd. Pickering. Uranium. CANDU.
3. Alouette. Anik. Telesat.
4. Operation Morning Light was the code name of the clean-up operation in the Barrens following the scattering of nuclear débris from the maverick Russian satellite Cosmos 954. The débris included particles of enriched U 235 which were scattered across 18,000 square miles of the Northwest Territories.
5. Kanata, Ont.
6. Telidon.
7. National Research Council. Spar Aerospace of Toronto. "Canadarm."

136. Outsiders

1. Athans is a water skier; the others, hockey players.
2. Bell is a swimmer; the others, boxers.
3. Crothers is a runner; the others, boxers.
4. Durelle is a boxer; the others, hockey players.
5. Elder is an equestrian; the others, hockey players.
6. Fontinato is a hockey player; the others, football players.
7. Gorman is a skater; the others, boxers.
8. Hayward is a speedboat racer; the others, rowers.
9. Irwin is a figure skater; the others, hockey personalities.
10. Jerome is a runner; the others, hockey players.
11. Kulai is a soccer player; the others, track performers.
12. Langford is a boxer; the others, golfers.
13. McCready is a wrestler; the others, shot-putters.
14. Nightingale is a figure skater; the others, hockey players.
15. O'Neill is a baseball player; the others, football players.
16. Purcell is a badminton star; the others, basketball players.
17. Russell is a gymnast; the others, swimmers.
18. Sherring is a marathon runner; the others, golfers.
19. Turcotte is a jockey; the others, shooters.
20. Urban is a tennis player; the others, badminton players.
21. Vaillancourt is an equestrian; the others, track performers.
22. Woolf is a jockey; the others, curlers.
23. Youngberg is a badminton star; the others, track performers.

137. Addagrams

A. GYMNASTICS.
B. SWIMMING.
C. ARCHERY.
D. WEIGHTLIFTING.
E. MARATHON.
F. SKATING.
G. WRESTLING.
H. TRACK AND FIELD.
I. BADMINTON.
J. BOBSLEDDING.
K. HOCKEY.
L. BASKETBALL.
M. CANOEING.
N. EQUESTRIAN.
O. FOOTBALL.
P. CURLING.
Q. BASEBALL.
R. BOWLING.
S. LACROSSE.
T. TENNIS.
U. RUGBY.

138. Boxing Ring

There are seven hidden names. The five boxers whose last names form the ring are (clockwise): Joey SANDULO, George CHUVALO, Jimmy McLARNIN, Frenchie BELANGER, Tommy BURNS. The two boxers whose first names appear in the ring are YVON Durelle and GALE Kerwin.

139. Gridiron Maze

1. Andreotti.
2. Cahill.
3. Ferraro.
4. Hendrickson.
5. Metras.
6. Oneschuk.
7. Paproski.
8. Parker.
9. Pulford.
10. Sazio.
11. Stukus.
12. Wydareny.

```
O
N   H E N D R I C K S O N
E               P               A
S   F E R R A R O               N
C               P U L F O R D   D
H   W Y D A R E N Y             R
U   C           O               E
K   A       S T U K U S O       O
    H P A R K E R               T
    I S A Z I O                 T
    L       M E T R A S         I
    L
```

140. Olympic Individualists

1. E.   4. C.
2. D.   5. A.
3. B.

141. Confusables

1. Track and field.
2. Anderson.
3. Tennis.
4. The Bauer brothers are Bobby and David. The Bentley brothers are Doug and Max. (Reg, Roy, and Scoop Bentley also played hockey; indeed Roy, Doug, and Max were perhaps the first three-brother act in the NHL.)
5. Boucher.
6. Track.
7. Petra Burka is the figure skater, Sylvia Burka the speed skater.

8. *Vice versa.* Bobby plays hockey, Bill played football.
9. No. The correct spellings are: Yvan Cournoyer and Alex Delvecchio.
10. Suzanne Eon is the synchronized swimmer. Mickey Ion played lacrosse and was a hockey referee. And Dave Keon plays hockey.
11. Ferguson. That is, John Ferguson and Ferguson Jenkins.
12. A. ii.   D. v.
    B. iii.   E. vi.
    C. iv.   F. i.
13. Speedboat racing.
14. The statement is correct. (Kim Lumsdon is the daughter of Cliff.)
15. Mahovlich.
16. Jean Potvin.
17. Vince.
18. Both are named Ron.
19. Judo.
20. Wrestler.

142. Some New Trophies

1. Lacrosse. Beers, a dentist and lacrosse player, helped formulate the laws of the game.
2. Hockey.
3. Boxer. George Chuvalo.
4. Equestrian. An equestrian club or association would be honoring dressage champions, Christilot Boylen and Jim Elder.
5. Swimmers. Nancy Garapick.
6. A round, white trophy would resemble a golf ball, and would honor champion golfer George Knudson.
7. Skiing. Two sisters, Kathy Kreiner and Laurie Kreiner.
8. Figure skater. Karen Magnussen.
9. A bullseye could represent shooting, a sport in which Susan Nattrass has excelled.
10. Basketball. Percy Page was a famous coach and promoter of the game.
11. Hockey. After Bobby Orr.
12. Track and field.
13. Bathing suit. Gus Ryder was an almost-legendary swimming instructor and Marilyn Bell's coach.
14. Auto racers burn rubber. Gilles Villeneuve was a leading auto racing driver.

143. Confusion at the NHL

1. Boston Bruins.
2. Buffalo Sabres.
3. Calgary Flames.
4. Chicago Black Hawks.
5. Colorado Rockies.
6. Detroit Red Wings.
7. Edmonton Oilers.
8. Hartford Whalers.
9. Los Angeles Kings.
10. Minnesota North Stars.
11. Montreal Canadiens.
12. New York Islanders.
13. New York Rangers.
14. Philadelphia Flyers.
15. Quebec Nordiques.
16. St. Louis Blues.
17. Toronto Maple Leafs.
18. Vancouver Canucks.
19. Washington Capitals.
20. Winnipeg Jets.

144. Sweater Numbers

1. Jean Béliveau.
2. King Clancy.
3. Gordie Howe. Bobby Hull, Ted Kennedy. Maurice Richard.
4. Bernie (Boom Boom) Geoffrion.
5. Maurice (The Rocket) Richard. (He also wore Number 9.)
6. Stan Mikita was born in Czechoslovakia, Borje Salming in Sweden.
7. Darryl Sittler. Frank Mahovlich.
8. Wayne Gretzky.

145. Sports Nicknames

1. I.	7. E.
2. J.	8. C.
3. F.	9. H.
4. K.	10. D.
5. A.	11. L.
6. G.	12. B.

146. Miscasting

1. Somers is a composer; the others are ballet personalities.
2. Haddad is a clothes designer; the others are variety performers.
3. Russell is a comedienne and singer; the others are theater people.
4. Yost is a TV host and film buff; the others are ballet dancers.
5. Kilbourn is an historian; the others are actors.
6. Moore is a theater man; the others are choral directors.
7. Phillips is a stage director; the others are pop singers.
8. Barris is a writer and interviewer; the others are comedians.
9. Snow is a painter; the others are theater personalities.
10. Strange is an announcer; the others are actors.

147. Guide to Plays

1. G.	8. K.
2. E.	9. I.
3. M.	10. N.
4. F.	11. B.
5. H.	12. J.
6. C.	13. A.
7. D.	14. L.

148. Music and Drama

1. B.	5. C.
2. C.	6. A.
3. B.	7. B.
4. A.	8. C.

149. Telecasting

1. Montreal. Toronto.
2. Percy Saltzman. Horn-rimmed glasses. His chalk in the air and catching it again (usually). Christie. Campbell.
3. CTV, or Canadian Television Network.
4. Colorcasting was permitted.
5. The regulatory commission is the Canadian Radio-Television and Telecommunications Commission (CRTC).
6. Cable Television.
7. Pay TV, or subscription television.

150. Entertainers Galore

1. C.	6. C.
2. F.	7. C.
3. C.	8. C.
4. B.	9. B.
5. A.	

151. Anyone Watching?

1. "Front Page Challenge." Panelists are

198

Pierre Berton, Betty Kennedy, and Gordon Sinclair.

2. All seven have been newscasters on the late-evening program that is now called "The National."

3. **A.** Roy Bonisteel.
   B. David Suzuki.
   C. Roy Campanella and Tiiu Leek.

4. Bruno Gerussi.

5. Second City TeleVision, a weekly, prime-time Canadian program seen across North America.

6. A fancy name for a television documentary produced by Harry Rasky.

7. Robert Homme, who plays the Friendly Giant on the popular children's program.

8. "Radisson."

9. "Quentin Durgens, M.P."

10. "Wojek." Dr. Morton Shulman.

11. Joyce Davidson.

12. Norm Perry.

13. Graham Kerr. Bobby Gimby.

14. "Hockey Night in Canada."

15. "This Hour Has Seven Days."

16. "Reach for the Top" and "Génie en Herbe."

152. The Rails

1. The Intercolonial was chartered in New Brunswick. It thus served the Maritimes and ultimately linked Halifax to Quebec. Canadian National Railways.

2. Edward VII. Pullman. Pullman.

3. Craigellachie, Eagle Pass, B.C. The wording on the plaque draws attention to the completion of the Canadian Pacific Railway.

4. He created the "vista-dome car" by fitting a passenger car with a roof-top cupola. CP introduced them in 1902 and they were popular until the First World War, especially on the Rocky Mountain run.

5. Canadian National Railways.

6. Alexander Graham Bell, pioneer in communications and transportation, died at his summer home at Baddeck, N.S., 2 Aug. 1922. Service was halted at the hour of his death two days later.

7. "Selkirks" were the largest locomotives in use in Canada. They were first built in Montreal in 1929,

and they continued in use until 1940. They weighed 190 tons and were semi-streamlined.

8. Invariably mentioned was and is "the Royal Blue train."

9. The old CNR acquired the new CN logo, created by Allan Fleming.

10. The *Rapido* connects Montreal and Toronto in just under five hours. The distance is 537 kilometres (335 miles). The even-faster *Turbo*, introduced in 1973, covers the same ground in just over four hours.

11. Canadian Pacific Railway became Canadian Pacific Limited to stress the diversified nature of its services, which are not limited to railways but extend to steamships, telecommunications, etc. The general manager who built the system was W.C. Van Horne.

12. VIA Rail Canada Inc.

13. Buster Keaton, the U.S. comedian. He continues to "ride the rails" in its sequel, *Buster Keaton Rides Again*, about the filming of *The Railrodder*.

153. Ships of Significance

1. F.	8. A.	14. Q.
2. S.	9. H.	15. J.
3. I.	10. D.	16. R.
4. M.	11. O.	17. C.
5. N.	12. E.	18. L.
6. P.	13. B.	19. G.
7. K.		

154. Wings Over the World

1. Alexander Graham Bell established the AEA at his summer home at Baddeck, N.S.

2. **A.** ii.
   B. iii.
   C. i.

3. F.W. (Casey) Baldwin.

4. "_____ Aces."

5. "Bush _____."

6. British Commonwealth Air Training Plan.

7. Trans-Canada Air Lines, the forerunner of Air Canada.

8. "High Flight."

9. Canadian Pacific Airlines, the forerunner of CP Air.

10. *North Star.*

11. The contract for the CF-105 — the famous *Avro Arrow* — was canceled

by the Conservative government of John G. Diefenbaker. This was a delta-winged, supersonic interceptor aircraft, the most advanced plane of its time.

12. Air Canada. Maple Leaf. Montreal.

155. Remarkable Women

1. Anna Brownell Jameson, author of *Winter Studies and Summer Rambles in Canada* (1838).
2. The Women's Institutes.
3. Laura Secord was a Loyalist woman who made a celebrated trek through the woods near Niagara to warn the British of an impending American attack.
4. Nellie McClung staged and starred in the Mock Parliament. Emily G. Murphy was the first police magistrate.
5. Emily Howard Stowe was the first woman to *practice medicine* in Canada, having graduated three years earlier from an American medical school and worked in Canada without authorization. Augusta Stowe Gullen, her daughter, was the first woman *to graduate from a school of medicine* in Canada.
6. Emily Carr. *Klee Wyck* was published in 1941.
7. Madeleine de Verchères.

156. Women's Firsts

1. D. Louise C. McKinney, Alberta, 1917.
2. C. Agnes Macphail, 1921.
3. E. Ellen Fairclough, 1957.
4. G. Jeanne Sauvé, 1980.
5. A. Cairine Wilson, 1930.
6. B. Pauline McGibbon, Ontario, 1973.
7. F. Pauline Jewett.

157. Female Emancipation

1. Manitoba was the first, Quebec was the last.
2. F.
3. True.
4. B.
5. D.

158. Line of Work

1. H. Long-time editor of *Chatelaine*.
2. F. First woman judge of the Supreme Court.
3. M. Outstanding cooking instructor.
4. K. Former radio, now television, personality.
5. B. Biographer who works in library "stacks."
6. J. Champion runner, now teacher.
7. A. Ballet dancer who works out at "the barre."
8. C. Sculptress who casts bronze statues at her metal-works.
9. D. Radio hostess and television panelist.
10. E. Author whose novels appear "in print."
11. G. Popular singer who is always in tune.
12. I. Actress who never misses her cues.
13. L. Marathon swimmer who is "in the swim."
14. O. First woman Speaker of the House of Commons.
15. N. Opera and concert singer.

159. Outstanding Women

1. ABELLA.   6. OSTRY.
2. ATWOOD.   7. REID.
3. FORRESTER.   8. TENNANT.
4. LIVESAY.   9. TYSON.
5. MURRAY.   10. WEILAND.

```
              R        W
F  O  R  R  E  S  T  E  R
              I        I
              D        L
M  A     M  U  R  R  A  Y
A  B              N  T
G  E  A  T  W  O  O  D  E
G  L  I  V  E  S  A  Y  N
I  L           T        N
E  A           R        A
            T  Y  S  O  N
                       T
```

Bonus Answer: MAGGIE (i.e., Margaret Trudeau).

160. Associations

1. A. The Union Jack, the official flag at the time.
   B. The Union Government, under Sir Robert Borden.
   C. Union Station, Toronto.
   D. Union Nationale, Duplessis's Quebec party.
2. "Injure."
3. N.S. "White." Miners are usually depicted black from coal-dust; the statue is white.
4. William Ford Coaker. Newfoundland.
5. Crafts.
6. The Canadian Labour Congress is an association of labour unions that dates from 1956. UIC is an abbreviation for Unemployment Insurance Commission.
7. The Canadian Union of Public Employees (CUPE). It does not include federal government employees, who are represented by the Public Service Alliance of Canada.
8. Anti-Inflation. "Day of Protest."
9. The first Monday of September, Labour Day.

161. Occupations

1. Novelist and poet.
2. Popular singer.
3. Novelist.
4. Former Conservative Cabinet minister.
5. Sports announcer.
6. Television host.
7. Marine scientist.
8. Journalist and editor.
9. An archbishop, a cardinal, and then a missionary.
10. Chief executive officer.
11. Chief executive officer.
12. An advertising executive.
13. Medical doctor.
14. Chansonnier, or singer-composer.
15. An editor and publisher.
16. Politician and parliamentary expert.
17. Clothes designer.
18. Comedienne.
19. Haida carver.
20. An essayist and lawyer.
21. Leading advocate.
22. Politician and former B.C. Premier.
23. Singer.
24. Poet and teacher.
25. Singer.
26. Television personality.
27. Novelist and translator.

162. Names in the News

Note: In filling in the blanks, other related answers are possible of course, as singers may also be composers, track- and field-stars could also be called athletes, etc. So some latitude is permitted in these answers.

1. Athlete.
2. Business executive.
3. Politician.
4. Performer, comic.
5. Football player.
6. Conductor, orchestra conductor.
7. Jockey.
8. Astronomer.
9. Conductor, choral conductor.
10. Track star, high jumper.
11. Broadcaster, newscaster, anchorman.
12. Judge, Supreme Court judge.
13. Labor leader.
14. Marathon swimmer.
15. Former hockey player.
16. Physicist.
17. Singer, opera singer.
18. Playwright.
19. Golfer.
20. Lawyer, politician.
21. Boxing personality, fight arranger.
22. Social worker, humanitarian.
23. Broadcaster.
24. Fur trader, factor. (It would be a shame not to include an entry under X just because few if any public figures have names beginning with the third-last letter of the alphabet.)
25. Singer, composer.
26. Wit, *bon-vivant*, writer, controversialist, comic, broadcaster, etc.

163. Through Foreign Eyes

1. B.   5. A.
2. B.   6. B.
3. B.   7. C.
4. C.   8. B.

164. Canadians Abroad

1. C.
2. D.
3. B. (The company is Brascan.)
4. C. (He died in China but first worked in Spain.)
5. C.
6. A.
7. D.
8. C.
9. D.
10. C.
11. A.
12. B.

---

165. Farewell!

1. C.
2. D.
3. E. Northern Quebec; *taavauvutut* across the Northwest Territories.
4. B.
5. A. Cree Indian farewell.